INSIDE THE MIND OF A
SCOUT

What Every Parent Wishes They Knew About
The Major League Scouting Process

JEREMY BOOTH

Ainsley & Allen Publishing

ISBN: 978-1-946694-77-5

All inquiries should be sent to info@insidethemindofascout.com

Acknowledgments

I am deeply grateful to my parents, Aaron and Joan, for birthing me directly into the game of baseball and the sacred spaces of clubhouses. Your unwavering support and love have propelled me forward every step of the way.

To my remarkable aunts, uncles, grandparents, and those close to me growing up who played an integral role in shaping my character during my formative years, I extend my heartfelt appreciation. You instilled in me invaluable lessons of work ethic, accountability, humility, honesty, directness, resiliency, commitment, and loyalty. I owe a debt of gratitude to a special group of family and friends—Andrew, Adam, Chris, Jodi, Derek, Renee, Kenya, Velma, Brian, Jason, Daniel, Matt, Erik, Tony, Andre, Armando, Dean, Sheila, Bernadette, Don, Michael, Patrick, Kevin, Ray C, John, Nick, Bonnie, Ryan, Dina, Ray, Andy, Neil, as well as my grandfathers, Marlowe and Everett. Your presence in my life has been profoundly influential.

To the mentors and teachers who generously shared their wisdom and guided me through every facet of the game that moves us all, I extend my deepest thanks. Jack Zduriencik, Bobby Heck, Ray Montgomery, Deron Johnson, Bruce Seid, Mark Snipp, Gordon Blakeley, Kevin Bootay, Dan Nellum, Kelcey Mucker, Arnold Brathwaite, Mike Rikard, Marc Tramuta, Joe Butler, Brian Bridges, Marc Delpiano, Bobby Evans, Junior Vizcaino, Jim Duquette, Joe Katuska, Danny Montgomery, Sean Johnson, David Post, Butch Baccala, Clarence Johns, Scott

Barnsby, Rickey Drexler, Tim O'Neil, Rich Morales, Tom McNamara, Tim and Maggie Corbin, Rob Cooper, Jay Uhlman, Derek Johnson, and Gabe Alvarez —your mentorship and expertise have been invaluable in shaping my journey.

To my honorary uncles throughout the game, who graciously imparted their vast knowledge whenever the opportunity arose, I extend my sincere appreciation. Eric Davis, Ken Medlock, Mike Garner, "Big Money" Robert Moore, Tony Phillips, Rickey Henderson, Dave Stewart, Ron Washington, Darryl Strawberry (who not only taught me how to dunk on my driveway rim when I was ten but also shared his wisdom), and Chris Brown—I am forever grateful for the wisdom you bestowed upon me.

Lastly, a special thank you to some educators I was blessed to learn from along the way. Jenny Cabrejas, who taught me never to doubt myself. Herb Hall, who kept me laughing when life wasn't all that funny. Bill Smith, who drilled into me what was ahead and refused any shortcuts. Franklin Memmer, who literally handed me the keys to the stars and told me to go find my place among them. Elaine Falk, who once upon a time told a seventeen-year-old All-American that one day when playing the game was over, he would be on Television and write books. And Jack Mize, who convinced me to write this book.

To all those who have touched my life and contributed to my journey as a baseball scout, your support, guidance, and belief in me have been immeasurable. This book stands as a testament to the collective efforts and profound impact you have had on my career and my passion for this timeless game. Thank you.

Table of Contents

Foreword

I am in the midst of Year 30 in Professional Baseball and a much better "Bob the Builder" than the Minor League player I was for a few minutes. Scouting kind of found me after my playing days when I needed an internship to finish my Sports Management degree. I was a Bird Dog/Associate Scout for the Milwaukee Brewers under former Miami Dade legend Demie Mainieri in South Florida for my internship. That experience led to a part-time role with Brewers, eventually leading to a full-time Area Scout opportunity with the Texas Rangers in 1995, covering four states in the southeast.

After four years with the Rangers, Jack Zduriencik and the Brewers came calling to be their East Coast Scouting Supervisor in October of 1999. The same Jack Zduriencik would eventually hire Jeremy with the Brew Crew. After eight Drafts and what most in the industry would say was a successful run, Ed Wade and the Houston Astros hired me to be the Amateur Scouting Director/Assistant GM in October 2007.

After running five Drafts that netted 25 Major League players, many of whom played pivotal roles in the Astros' 2017 World Series Championship, I was sent to scout free agency in August 2012. Soon after, Andrew Friedman and the Tampa Bay Rays hired me as a Special Assignment Scout. Ironically, Friedman was the top GM target of the Astros' new owner, Jim Crane.

Friedman departed for the Los Angeles Dodgers in the fall of 2014. Matt Silverman, who was already club President, took over the reins of the Rays Baseball Operations and promoted me to Special Assistant to the General Manager. Mine is a functional role, not the honorary title sometimes bestowed upon former players. Many of my responsibilities are high leverage evaluating for trades, the amateur Draft, International free agents, our minor league players, and our Major League club.

I met Jeremy briefly while he was still an Area Scout with the Twins and me with the Brewers. Our relationship grew once he joined the Brewers staff as a Regional Scouting Supervisor, and I was a new Scouting Director in Houston. We found ourselves in similar ballparks more frequently as I was Scouting more on a national scope. He was now working for Jack Zduriencik, who had been my Scouting Director with the Brewers, creating natural conversations.

Jeremy's energy, presence, and competitiveness were always felt at the ballpark. He was always inquisitive about all things Scouting but never crossed the line of asking my opinion about players in that year's Draft. If it was about players, it was about players from previous Drafts so that he could learn from my evaluation process of such players. My involvement with the Buck O'Neil Professional Baseball Scouts & Coaches Association started in the fall of 2008 with an invitation from Clarence Johns, my East Coast Supervisor with the Astros, who helped put us on at least one same team.

I think our relationship got legs when neither was "renewed." You know, the new age way of saying "fired." You learn a lot about yourself and others in Scout Free Agency. You spend real time reflecting because you finally exhale and are no longer on the baseball hamster wheel that runs much longer than the MLB season. There is no off-season, just ask my wife, Nicole. I had already built, but now it was time for Jeremy to build something—PROGRAM 15.

The professional Scouting community has long relied upon summer showcases to bring the best players to one spot. Jeremy saw inequity and exploitation and had a vision of a better way to give opportunities to more players due to their talent and not just their parents' wallets. Not long after his PROGRAM 15 launch, Jeremy invited me to be a part of his Advisory Board which has netted me one pair of New Balance sneakers. All joking aside, I was happy to be a sounding board for him as he built it out because I believed in his vision that would service young baseball players looking to play beyond high school.

It's been fun to watch Jeremy and PROGRAM 15 continue to grow. He's become what I believe are the most valuable people in our game, the "Hybrid:" college educated, played profession-ally, old school baseball foundation, and a growth mindset. With his knowledge and understanding of all the new tech and data that has entered the baseball world in the last ten years, he's learned much faster than he would have otherwise. Mixing that with the fact that he knows what is applicable from all that's being counted nowadays is precious. It puzzles me that a Major League organization has not swept him up in the past few years because he's a plug-and-play Scouting Director or Farm Director that can lead people from his experience and continued growth since his days with the Mariners.

You never have to wonder what Jeremy is thinking, which is good for most. Seriously, he is always ultra-informed with his opinions and educated about whatever is at hand. And on the rare occasion he is not, Jeremy is comfortable saying, "I don't know," which means he will be up to speed the next time you talk to or see him. More than anything else, Jeremy is a giver and a sharer. So, his undertaking of this book's subject matter lines up with him very well but, more importantly, will benefit those who read this book to get a perspective that very few have exposure to.

Bobby Heck
Special Assistant to Baseball President & General Manager
Tampa Bay Rays Baseball Club

Introduction

Stepping Up to the Plate

Imagine this: you're sitting in the bleachers at a high school baseball game, and the energy of the game is electric. As you scan the crowd, your eyes land on a guy sitting behind home plate who seems out of place, and you can't help but be curious. He's got a radar gun, a notepad, and a stopwatch, and he's glued to the action on the field. This is no ordinary spectator; he's a pro baseball scout.

Who is he here to see? Is he watching my kid? Your eyes dart back and forth between the scout and the game as he carefully observes each pitch, each swing, and each sprint around the bases. He raises his radar gun, measures the speed of a fastball, and scribbles something in his notepad. The stopwatch clicks as he records a player's time sprinting from home to first base. You wonder what he's writing–is he taking note of strengths and weaknesses, or does he see some hidden potential?

Let's be honest. As a parent, seeing a scout at your kid's game gets your heart racing. Is this it? The moment that sends your kid toward their dream? You think about the endless hours of practice, late-night skill sessions, and sacrifices made for the love of the game. This scout is a glimmer of hope, a shot at turning that passion up a notch.

But with hope comes fear. What if the scout misses your kid's potential? What if it's not his best game? Your mind is racing as you quietly hope your child shows something that will stick with the scout.

You keep peaking at the scout throughout the game, searching for clues in his expressions. Is he impressed? Disappointed? You can't tell! The stakes soar with every play, and you're holding your breath, praying this is the day that changes everything for your child's baseball journey.

I've been that scout, spending endless hours watching and evaluating young baseball talent. I know the emotions parents and players go through when a scout is in the house – the anticipation, the excitement, and, yeah, the anxiety.

I wrote this book to ease some of that anxiety by giving you an exclusive, behind-the-scenes look into the world of baseball scouting. I will break down what's going on in a scout's head when they're hunting for talent, from stepping on the field to making the final call. You'll learn how we evaluate players' skills, character, and growth potential.

I'm pulling back the curtain to offer valuable insights and practical tips, helping you navigate the world of baseball scouting with confidence and clarity – from finding and assessing players to what scouts want in specific positions. We'll dive into what makes a player successful, the power of mental and emotional resilience, and the vital role of hard work and dedication in chasing the dream. Plus, I'll bust some myths and misconceptions about scouting, giving you a real understanding of the challenges and opportunities ahead.

I want you to know that I get it – the passion, commitment, and sacrifice both players and parents put into chasing baseball greatness. Success is built on hard work, dedication, and grit. "Inside the Mind of a Scout" is your go-to guide for the knowledge and tools to make smart choices and the encouragement to stay passionate about the game, embrace feedback, and always aim for progress.

The road to success will be challenging, but with the right mindset, support, and guidance, you'll be ready to tackle the ultra-competitive world of baseball.

Know this: I'm in your corner, rooting for your success.

Major League organizations start identifying and evaluating players as early as high school freshman year. Before that, I tell parents and players to focus on enjoying the game of baseball and determine if there's a genuine passion for playing at the high school level.

While having fun, prepare for the next level and never stop building those skills. You never know when a chance to show off that talent might arise, so always be ready and keep grinding to improve.

Remember that baseball is not just about getting discovered by scouts but also about loving the journey and the game itself.

Embrace mentorship and guidance – that's gold. The most successful scouts I know have leaned on the wisdom and support of mentors throughout their careers. I've been fortunate to have seasoned pros give me priceless insights along my journey.

Early in my scouting career with the Minnesota Twins, I was at an event, sitting near the bottom of the stands, grinding and sweating, doing my thing. I just kept feeling like I was being watched, feeling these eyes on me from behind. I turned around and saw this guy looking at me and smiling from the top of the stands. Every time I looked back, he was watching me. Finally, I approached him, and he said, "I'm Kevin Bootay. I used to be a Twin. I'm the West Coast supervisor with the Rangers now. You need anything, let me know."

I came to learn that Kevin Bootay was keeping an eye on me for Deron Johnson, watching out for and taking care of me to make sure I stayed headed in the right direction. "KB" and "DJ" were members of the Buck O'Neil Scouts Association, the organization founded in honor of the legendary Hall of Famer Buck O'Neil, who was the first African American to coach in the Major Leagues and one of the first full-time scouts. They were making sure that, as a young scout, I had the mentorship I needed.

I was introduced to "The Buck" by Deron Johnson. My first time attending, Jack Zduriencik, the Brewers Scouting Director who hired me before he went on to become General Manager of the Mariners, was sitting in the front row. It was very interesting to watch the support from that group of people who didn't have to be there.

Over the years, along with Jack, Deron, and Kevin, a whole network of guys, including Danny Montgomery, Bobby Heck, Ray Montgomery, and Stevie Williams, made sure I was covered from the beginning. They not only taught me about the mechanics of scouting but, more importantly, they taught me about accountability, resilience, focus, integrity, lessons, and conviction.

Finding mentors for your player (and even yourself) can make a difference. Surround yourself with people who can give constructive feedback, share their experiences, and push you to reach your full potential.

Now, let's step up to the plate, swing for the fences, and jump into this mysterious world of baseball scouting. Together, we'll uncover the secrets, strategies, and insights that can fuel your baseball journey and bring you closer to achieving your dreams. Welcome to "Inside the Mind of a Scout." Let the adventure begin!

Chapter 1

The Scout's Role in Baseball

Ted Williams hit the nail on the head when he said, "Without question, the hardest single thing to do in sports is to hit a baseball."

Now, ask any seasoned baseball scout, and they'll tell you that finding players who can do just that at the pro level is just as tough.

I actually think it's even tougher. I say that because when you sign or draft a player, you lose control over their progress. It's really up to the player and the development department. When someone like Ted Williams is in the batter's box, he can control his swing and body to make contact, but as a scout, you no longer have that control once you sign a player—so, finding a true big leaguer? That's gotta be the hardest thing to do.

At the heart of every professional baseball scout lies a deep, unwavering commitment to the game. Their love for baseball fuels their endless hours on the road, sleepless nights, and pressure-packed decisions. That passion drives them to hunt for talent and help players reach for the stars.

The Scout's Decision-Making Process

"You know, as soon as you submit your report – you're wrong."

That's what my scouting supervisor, Tim O'Neil, said to me on my very first day with the Minnesota Twins as I was trying to figure out the scouting report computer system.

What did he mean by that? Well, if you think somebody is going to be an All-Star – he probably won't. And if you think you found a guy who is going to be a fringe player – he's probably better than you think.

Scouting is not an exact science, and it's impossible to get it right every time. But we never stop trying.

During my time with the Twins, I learned a lot about finding the balance between conviction, humility, and accountability needed to be a great scout.

Confidence and conviction are absolute requirements for a baseball scout. You have to be able to trust your gut because your decisions can make or break a player's future and the team's success. I get how parents could sometimes misinterpret a scout's confidence as aloofness or arrogance. Please understand that their unwavering demeanor is vital for the high-stakes nature of the job.

Guys like Deron Johnson, Bruce Seid, Sean Johnson, and Joe McIlvaine taught me that while conviction is essential, it needs to be tempered with humility and a willingness to step back and reevaluate one's approach.

They would say, "Don't ever let anybody talk you off your conviction if you believe in a player. You might not get the grades right, and that's okay. But if you think a guy can play and he's gonna be a big leaguer, and you believe in him, don't let someone else talk you out of it." They also taught me always to be willing to change my perspective based on what I see.

I remember the time I was with Sean Johnson in Cary, North Carolina. I had been there a couple of days, and we were catching up on some of the players we were seeing on the field that day. He points out a player and says with conviction, "This guy is a seven." Now, when you assign a role seven, you're projecting that this guy is a future All-Star. I looked at him with a raised eyebrow and said, "I got him as a six." We went back and forth until the guy came up to the plate. We stopped talking to get ready to argue our position on every nuance of his at-bat as we watched the guy swing and miss on three pitches in a row. Sean looks at me and says, "OK, maybe he's a six." Turned out we were both wrong, and the player turned out to be a deuce.

Those kinds of moments provided me with some simple but powerful lessons.

Being a great scout requires a sharp eye for talent, a deep knowledge of the game, and the hustle to search every corner of the country and beyond for the future stars of baseball. I have to be part detective, part analyst, and part risk-taker. For me and probably any scout you talk to, there's nothing like finding the next Mike Trout or Mookie Betts and watching them soar.

Of course, those guys are easy examples to use now, but Mike Trout was actually drafted after Randal Grichuk in the 2009 MLB Draft, 25th overall as the Angels' compensation pick. There was some strategy involved there by the Angels, but still, he was after Grichuk. You know, most teams wouldn't admit it, but not many had them in the first round of their draft boards. I was in the Milwaukee Brewers' draft room at the time, and well, we definitely weren't picking Trout at 26 that year. Even the Angels couldn't have predicted he'd breeze through the minors and into the big leagues so quickly, let alone have the career he's had.

Now, Mookie Betts – that's another interesting case. A fifth-round pick in 2011, he wasn't really a household name then. But Mike Rikard, now the VP of Scouting with the Red Sox, saw something special. He recognized that Mookie had the tools, upside, and make up – the whole package.

Trout and Betts were drafted for their future potential and ended up outshining all those picks ahead of them. Just goes to show you that scouting is about spotting the diamonds in the rough.

So yeah, hitting a baseball and discovering the next great player both require a rare and unique degree of skill, perseverance, and fortitude. But for those who live and breathe the game, the rewards are well worth the effort.

If you could peek inside a scout's mind, you would see a delicate dance between rigorous quantitative analysis and the fine-tuned intuition that separates a great scout from a good scout. Great scouts will scrutinize the data thrown at them, leaving no stone unturned in their quest to find true talent. But they also trust their gut instinct, tapping into their finely-honed intuition to uncover the hidden gems others might overlook. This artful balance between data-driven analysis and intuitive insight is what makes a scout's decision-making process truly remarkable.

In the pro baseball world, an organization's strength comes from the team working together to find, evaluate, draft, sign, and develop players. Everyone has to be in sync, from scouting to data-driven analysis to front-office personnel to player development. And scouting is at the heart of it all.

A great scout is more than just someone who writes reports. They use their eyes, ears, experience, game knowledge, and every bit of information they can get their hands on to make smart observations and analytical assessments. They follow players over time, gathering as much intel as possible about their tools, skills, and intangibles.

I've spent countless hours traveling, watching games, and evaluating players, searching for that diamond in the rough who has the potential to become a future MLB star. Raw talent alone isn't enough; I'm also looking for work ethic, mental toughness, and other intangibles that can make or break a player's career and organizational direction for years to come.

Spending all this time and doing all this work means you have to know your players. Jack Zduriencik was absolutely adamant that there were no surprises. One day, Jack flew to LA to meet me so we could see Michael Conforto. I had an extensive history with Jack, and we are close, so this wasn't the usual occurrence where a scout might be nervous with his GM.

It turns out that Jack and I were staying in the same hotel. We scheduled a time to meet in the lobby and discussed where to eat before going to the ballpark. Now might be a good time to tell you that Jack is a bit particular, but he and I pretty much share the same brain on players and everything else, so we moved in sync.

On the way to lunch, we were talking about the Big League club, the weather, and pretty much anything except the guy we were about to go see. Then out of the blue, in mid-acceleration on the gas, and after a comment about a sandwich and restaurant, he says without missing a beat, "So what you got on Conforto?" I looked over at him, and he was just looking at me for a reaction. This isn't my first day with Jack, so I'm ready and answer him directly. He hears my answer, takes it in without much further comment, and we go to the park. Jack was beautiful with the ambush questions, but the overarching point is always to be ready. It matters because life-altering decisions are made based on the work a scout puts in.

But it's not just about data collection. A scout's real value is in using that info properly and creatively to plot a course to success. That's a very human thing; there is no computer algorithm that matches a skilled scout's creativity and strategic thinking. Anyone who tells you otherwise is wrong.

Professional Scout vs. College Coach/Recruiter

Before we get too deep into the core of scouting, I have to make crystal clear the differences between the type of player a professional scout is looking for and what a college coach is after.

Both, of course, are on the hunt for talent, but their criteria and ultimate goals are often very different.

Professional scouts focus on identifying players with the potential to compete at the highest level of the sport—Major League Baseball. They evaluate prospects based on their raw athletic ability, physical tools, and growth potential. Professional scouts are often willing to take a chance on a player who may be a bit rough around the edges but has a high ceiling for development. This means they're ready to invest time and resources into molding these young athletes into MLB-ready players, even if it takes a few years in the minor leagues. POTENTIAL is the key focus when evaluating a big-league prospect.

The goal of true scouting is never about "now." It is always about the future. As players progress through the game of baseball, they develop at every level. It's the scout's job to determine a player's potential of what they will become when the draft comes around their senior year.

Big League clubs split their domestic professional scouting operations into two separate departments – Pro and Amateur.

Pro Scouts. A pro scout focuses on evaluating talent at the professional level, including minor and major league players. They might be looking for potential trade targets or free agents to improve their team's roster.

Amateur Scouts. An amateur scout is responsible for identifying and evaluating talent at the high school and college levels. They attend games, analyze players' skills, and assess their potential to play professional baseball.

For the purposes of this book, when I say *Scout*, I'm talking about **Amateur Scouts**. They're the ones who find those hidden gems in the draft, looking for players with the right combination of skills, athleticism, and character to succeed in the big leagues.

On the other hand, for college coaches, it's often all about the "now." They are searching for players who can contribute to their program's success right away and are looking for more polished athletes who are ready to compete at the collegiate level. College coaches must also consider a player's academic performance and how they will fit into their team's culture. Since college baseball is not just about athletics but also about education, coaches need players who can balance the demands of school and sports. As a side note, professional scouts cannot stand when college coaches are referred to as "scouts."

Here's the bottom line. My job as a professional scout is to paint a picture of what a player can and will become.

Recognizing and understanding these differences can help you to adjust your approach accordingly. A player aiming for a professional career should focus on sharpening their physical tools and showcasing their potential for growth. However, if college baseball is the goal, emphasizing current abilities, academic achievements, and character traits that demonstrate you're a team player is key.

Understanding the Major League Scouting System

The Major League scouting process is a well-organized machine designed to discover promising players, evaluate their skills and potential, and help teams make informed decisions regarding player acquisitions through the draft, trades, or free agency.

Following is a breakdown of how the process typically works.

Every MLB team has a dedicated scouting department consisting of a director of scouting, national crosscheckers, area scouts, and international scouts. These individuals work collaboratively to cover various regions and levels of play, including high school, college, and international leagues.

Associate Scouts – Bird Dogs

You may have heard the term Associate Scout or, as they are more commonly known, "Bird Dogs." They were not full-time employees of Major League organizations. This role was often filled by local high school and travel team coaches looking for hidden gems and players that other scouts may have overlooked. Bird Dogs would earn a fee if a club signed a player based on their recommendation. While this role remains in a few clubs, most professional scouts have replaced this concept by developing a network of trusted sources that help them with player identification at the grassroots level.

When I first started as a scout, I was an associate scout for the Philadelphia Phillies while coaching the Sussex Skyhawks in the Can-Am League. I reported to the legendary independent league scout Mal Fichman. Since I would see everyone in the league, I'd recommend players from independent baseball to be signed by the Phillies. I didn't actually write reports, however—just word-of-mouth evaluations. My first report writing happened for James Gamble and the then Global Scouting Bureau, which placed players across the planet in whatever league their talent level allowed.

Area Scouts

Area Scouts are full-time employees of Major League clubs. These scouts are the unsung heroes, tirelessly pounding the pavement, attending high school, college, and travel team games in designated territories, which usually cover a specific state or region (for example, South Texas).

Area Scouts are responsible for evaluating the players they learn about through their network or local bird dog. They compile a list of potential prospects for the draft, keeping their eyes peeled for players with raw talent and the potential to make it big.

Having a wealth of knowledge and expertise about the players in their area, area scouts can provide valuable insights to their organizations in the drafting process. Their dedication and hard work in identifying and evaluating players is critical to the success of their clubs.

Keep an eye out for Area Scouts. Make sure your player keeps working hard and stays dedicated. Area Scouts are watching, and you never know when an opportunity might arise.

Regional Cross-Checkers

Regional Cross-Checkers are the bridge between local scouting efforts and the national level. They are responsible for ensuring that their region's scouting efforts are aligned with their national organization's strategy. These scouts oversee a group of Area Scouts in a particular region, such as the West Coast, Midwest, or Northeast.

Regional Cross-Checkers swing by to catch a game and get a firsthand look at the players their Area Scouts have been raving about. They evaluate players and provide a broader perspective on the players in their region to their organizations to identify potential prospects for the draft.

National Cross-Checkers

National Cross-Checkers are the second in command for an organization. These scouts have their eyes on players eligible for the amateur draft, including prospects from Canada to Puerto Rico. Using all the information gathered by area and regional scouts, national cross-checkers make sure the best of the best are on the radar for their MLB team.

National Cross-Checkers often travel far and wide to watch the most highly touted prospects in action, ensuring no potential superstar slips through the cracks.

These scouts focus primarily on finding players for the first three to five rounds of the draft, where their organization is looking to secure future stars. They will try to see as many players as possible and may also evaluate players to be considered in later rounds, often looking at college programs or specific matchups to maximize their time.

Scouting Directors

Scouting Directors have the final say in player selections for Major League organizations. Their attendance at a game signifies a high level of interest in a player, but the absence of a Scouting Director does not necessarily mean a player is not being considered for selection.

Some players have been selected despite not being seen by a Scouting Director due to unforeseen circumstances such as injuries or weather conditions. However, if a Scouting Director is watching a player, it's a sign that the player is in heavy consideration to be drafted somewhere in the first three rounds.

Scouting Directors lead their team into the draft and have the final say on every pick. They will typically see around 200 players; from those, they select just 20. Ultimately, they're responsible for every player the organization drafts, regardless of who the area scout or cross-checker is.

When leading the draft, the Scouting Director is the one making the decisions. Even though the area scout gets some credit for finding and signing a player, the Scouting Director is recognized for guiding the selection and signing process. But you know what? If a player doesn't pan out or something goes wrong, they also get the blame.

While Scouting Directors may attend games during a player's junior year, it's more likely to happen by accident when they are at the game to see a senior prospect who is also on the team. Scouting Directors may be present at a few events in the summer, but they are typically busy preparing for the upcoming draft in July. It's more likely that high school players will see Scouting Directors during their senior year, particularly in the fall leading into the spring season or during the spring season itself. Because they have limited time, they focus on players they believe will be worth the investment.

As a rule of thumb, if a Scouting Director is present at a game, it's a sign of heavy consideration for selection. High school players should focus on showcasing their skills during their senior year and staying dedicated to their game. Even if you don't see a Scouting Director at the games, keep working hard and striving toward your goals because anything is possible in the world of baseball.

International Scouting

International scouts are all about finding and evaluating talent outside the US. They're key to discovering and signing players from countries with strong baseball traditions, like the Dominican Republic, Cuba, Venezuela, Japan, and up-and-coming baseball nations.

Many of today's top MLB players come from outside the United States, and international scouting has played a crucial role in their success. Without these scouts, players like David Ortiz, Shohei Ohtani, Fernando Tatis Jr., and Ronald Acuña Jr. might never have had a chance to showcase their skills on the world stage.

The life of a professional baseball scout is not all glamour and glitz. There are many hot days and late nights at the ballpark and endless player analysis. Those few hours of games where we get to hunt for prospects are often sandwiched between days of long and uncomfortable road trips.

I remember scouting for the Mariners. I got on a very small United Airlines regional jet out of Houston, Texas—definitely not built for my 6'5" frame. As soon as I board, I see Bobby Heck sitting in seat 1A.

He looked at me and said, "So, you want to be a cross-checker?"

Translation: "Do you really want to crisscross back and forth across the country, crammed into tight seats of a narrow plane?"

When scouting is in your blood, the only answer is, "LET'S GO!"

The amount of traveling from ballpark to ballpark is nuts. One year, I did 240 days on the road.

Routing efficiency often plays little, if any, part in determining a scout's travel schedule. It's all about the urgency of when and where you can see a player.

I've gone from Texas to the Dominican Republic, back to Texas for a day, then to Alaska, and back to Texas for another day before heading to Cape Cod.

But to a scout, the thrill of the hunt and finding that hidden gem makes it worth it.

Parents, take inspiration from the scout's tireless pursuit of talent. Embrace the grind, savor the journey, and never stop pushing your player to be their best. Because whether they make it to the pros or not, the experience will shape their life success.

Chapter 2

What is He Talking About?
Scout to English Dictionary

I understand that when parents listen to scout's conversations or try to read a scouting report, it may seem like we're speaking in a secret code. We're not intentionally trying to confuse anyone; we just have our own way of communicating, like how teenagers have their own lingo. We use phrases like "role," "exit velo," "WHIP," or "OFP," and to us, they make perfect sense.

That's why I put together this handy "Scout to English" guide. It breaks down some common terms that scouts use when evaluating players and translates them into terms everyone can understand. If you hear us talking about a player's "makeup," for example, you know we're not referring to his appearance.

Introduction to Scouting Phraseology

In the next chapter, we'll get into the fundamentals of the Five Tools and the 20-80 system that scouts use to grade players. But first, you need to get a sense of the language used to truly understand how to translate those evaluations.

Scouts are required to be very observant and must use standard phraseology in their reports. **These descriptive phrases support the reasoning behind their grades and provide context and**

supporting evidence. If a player is graded as a 60 future hitter (we'll get into what that means shortly), the scout must note the supporting evidence for why that grade was awarded.

The synergy between the report writer (scout) and the report reader (front office, crosschecker, or director) is critical to avoiding miscommunication. A reader should be able to visualize the player, their potential, and their role simply from a scout's report. If a scout takes liberties in their writing or creates new words, it could lead to a costly lesson in misinterpretation.

Words like "good," "great," "excellent," and others are not used in scouting. There is no such thing as a "good runner" or "great" power. And the word "plus" has a very specific meaning. The symbols (+) or (++) also have very specific meanings. I don't use these words and symbols liberally when I want to praise a player.

A scout can lose credibility, and even their job, if they're not careful with their choice of descriptive words. The numbers and the words they correspond to must be consistent.

Using simple, concise language to accurately describe a player's abilities and potential in reports enables it to be easily understood by those making decisions based on a scout's evaluations.

Scouting has hundreds of words and phrases with very specific meanings because it's crucial that everyone in the organization understands exactly what a scout means when saying a batter has a "closed" stance, is "late exit out of the box," or has a "clean arm action."

Let's examine some common, descriptive phrases that scouts use in reports.

Hitting Phraseology

Balance: Signs of balance may include a still head, a hitter whose feet are "in the ground," a player with a good center of gravity, and is under control when the swing is finished.

Bat Path: The route the bat takes from the stance to the load and through the strike zone.

Bat Stays in the Zone: The length of time that the bat stays in the hitting zone as it moves through the critical part of the swing (near contact).

Casting: When a player's swing gets long, the arms extend early in the swing, and the player loses strength and leverage.

Extension: A hitter with great extension will have the arms and bat extended through the swing, primarily after contact.

Gap to Gap: A guy who usually hits doubles and produces extra-base hits and RBIs.

Guess Hitter: A hitter who has to guess the pitch type to be successful. They have difficulty making mid-swing adjustments based on pitch speed and location.

Head Movement: Easier to see when using a reference point behind the player. Does the player keep their head relatively still, or does the head bounce down and up?

Head Pulls Off: When the head and eyes don't see the ball through contact. Usually, the hitter is trying too hard to generate power, and the head pulls away at contact.

In and Out of the Zone: The swing plane is down and back up: such that the barrel of the bat is barely ever in the hitting zone.

Knob to Catcher: The angle of the bat is such that the knob of the bat is pointing down and toward the catcher.

Leverage: The hitter's swing is such that the ball has traveled deep enough, and the hitter's body is in position to be used to exert maximum force on the baseball.

Lift: A hitter whose swing path through contact and body position at contact is conducive to generating home runs.

Light Tower Power: A hitter that doesn't just hit home runs, but their power generates a high arching loft that almost matches the height of the lights.

Loft Power: Another way to define a hitter that hits high, towering home runs that generate some hang time.

Load / Trigger: How the hands move into position and how the body prepares when the ball is about to be released.

Long Swing: The bat takes a long route, usually with premature extension, before it reaches the point of contact.

On Plane: The swing matches the incoming trajectory of the pitch. flat w/ slight lift. (i.e., level).

Pitch Recognition: When a hitter consistently struggles to identify pitch type. You can see a hitter lunge, be late, or be off balance, and it is sometimes the root cause of poor timing.

Plate Coverage: How much of the strike zone and hitting zone the hitter can cover with his barrel.

Rhythm and Timing: The player's ability to effortlessly get into sync with the incoming pitch and properly anticipate when to begin their swing.

Separation: The segment of the swing where the hands load back and create distance away from the front foot.

Short Swing: The bat takes a more efficient path, more direct to the ball. Players with short swings have a better chance of catching up to higher pitch velocity.

Stance: Square, closed, open, wide, narrow, tall, crouched – the hitter's starting position.

Stays Inside the Ball: A hitter who uses his hands well. The hands don't get away from his body, resulting in lost leverage. The hands stay compact and closer to the body than the ball gets.

Stride: Front foot action: length of stride, long, short, up and down, leg kick, toe tap, no stride.

Swing Plane: Level, down, uppercut.

Torque: When something twists or builds up potential energy to be released.

Fielding Phraseology

Active: A player who is constantly moving, rarely flat-footed, rarely lazy, and exudes energy.

Ball Runs or Tails: The throws are moving, not a good quality. Want straight, on-line throws – direct to the target.

Body Control: The ability of a player to move explosively while maintaining balance and control.

Can Throw from Anywhere on the Field: Player can field balls to their left or right; they don't always have to be in an optimal position. This usually relates to OF as well, being able to make any throw near the wall, and the field is not too big for them.

Carry: The ball's ability to maintain its velocity over a large distance. Balls without carry die out toward the end. A great way to see carry is the way the ball "skips" off the turf. Does it skip and dribble, or does it skip and JUMP off the ground? This is the result of the player creating backspin on the ball.

Feet Underneath Him: The thrower is under control, balanced.

Gets Rid of It: The fielder has no unnecessary additional footwork and is highly efficient in quickly getting the ball out of their hands.

Good Breaks off Bat: The player is already moving in the right direction off the bat, and it doesn't take them long to figure out where they will need to be to make the play.

Has Touch and Feel: The thrower is accurate and can make long throws and short throws without accuracy issues.

Makes the Routine Play: Not great, not bad. Nothing spectacular, but the defender is solid and consistent.

Needs to Stay Behind the Ball: The thrower is getting on the side of the ball, so the ball is moving and not getting a good 4-seam straight spin.

On line: The throws are accurate, rarely pulling the recipient off their base and through a cutoff man if necessary.

Stays Above the Ball: Staying above the ball means the ball is thrown with a downward trajectory, and the thrower is comfortable throwing through a cut.

Takes Good Angles: Usually in relation to OF, the OF gets good reads on where the ball is going and takes a direct angle to the ball, resulting in a higher percentage chance they make the catch.

Baserunning Phraseology

Better Underway: The player doesn't have instant acceleration in the first few steps, but once they run a longer distance, their speed becomes evident.

Can Score from 2B: Serviceable runner that isn't a liability; nothing special.

Choppy: Short, little steps when running.

Closing Speed: Usually in relation to an OF; player does not become hesitant as they get closer to making the catch, and they turn it to another level.

Disruptive: Player constantly does things that make a defense uncomfortable: stealing bases, taking extra bases, taking large leads, and being aggressive.

Dynamic: Energetic, effective, can do it all.

Easy: Running comes easy to them, and they are loose.

Fast Twitch: Player is explosive, and likely everything they do on the field is explosive.

Gets Down the Line: Good home-to-first runner, puts pressure on D.

Good Reads: Understands the game, can see the trajectory of thrown balls well, and makes decisions quickly to run or stay.

Has Another Gear: He's not only fast, but as you continue watching him run, he keeps getting faster. This becomes even more evident on triples, for example.

Late Exit with Finish to Swing: The player's swing has a pronounced finish that causes the player to get out of the box slowly.

Late Exit with Power Finish: Same.

Long Strides: Big steps, covers a lot of ground with each stride.

On a Bunt: A notation given to a home-to-first time, where the batter bunted. This affects their time since there was no finish to the swing – usually resulting in much faster times.

On the Turn: A notation given to a home-to-first time, where the runner ran hard, but he took a wide angle before touching first base to turn for a double. This obviously affects the time.

Pulled Up: A notation given to a home-to-first time where the runner didn't run hard all the way through the bag. Maybe the runner was thrown out by 5-10 feet and stopped running hard, affecting their time.

Quick Out of the Box: Gets bat down quickly after contact and begins running.

Station to Station: Not a liability, but nothing special.

Turns It on When He Smells a Hit: These players sometimes play up or down to the level of competition and have better tools than what they show day in and day out.

Watches Ball out of Box: Too busy watching the ball to gain ground towards first base.

Pitching Phraseology

Arm Action: The way a pitcher's arm "works" – from the path it travels to effort level, looseness, etc.

Command: The ability to throw strikes within the strike zone and hit specific targets from the catcher.

Control: The ability to throw strikes.

Cut: When the ball moves glove side; a RHP's ball "cuts" from his perspective into an LHH.

Depth: Describes the vertical break that a pitch gets; a pitch with a lot of "depth" is breaking downward, vertically, in a very favorable fashion.

Downhill Plane: When the angle that the pitch travels from the mound to the plate is traveling at a noticeably more downward angle than a usual pitch trajectory; often, a tall pitcher with a high release point can generate this.

Easy, Effortless: This is a positive; it doesn't mean the pitcher isn't trying; it just comes naturally. The arm isn't going through a violent process every pitch.

Falls Off: A pitcher who finishes off balance, and his momentum takes him off the mound.

Head Whack, Head Jerk: A pitcher whose head physically whacks, jerks, or moves violently at release; it is a bad sign and a very negative comment, but not always a deal-breaker.

Hides Ball: A pitcher that uses his body, alignment on the rubber, and delivery to not allow the hitter to see the ball in his hand until release.

Late Life, Late Action: A pitch that comes out of the hand similar to others and doesn't reveal its break until later in the pitch trajectory; these pitches are difficult to hit since the hitter has to make a split-second decision.

Life: A ball that is not straight and often has late action and late movement; it is "alive" and moving; a ball with life often has high spin.

Loops, Loopy: A pitch's break (usually a breaking ball) that is easily detected out of the hand by a batter; it does not travel in the same "tunnel" or trajectory as a fastball and noticeably travels upward in trajectory before it begins to break down.

Max Effort: A pitcher who looks like he has to use every ounce of his being to achieve velocity; he may even verbally grunt at release; over a 162-game season, this violence is extremely tough on these guys; therefore, max effort arms are usually closers or short relievers at best.

Loose: To not muscle up the arm, to let the arm be free; pitching is very violent on the arm, and we want it loose and easy.

On Line: A pitcher who is properly balanced, and delivery travels in a straight line to the catcher.

Pitchability: A pitcher that knows what he is doing, can locate, change speeds, is in the zone, is not raw or new to pitching, and can execute.

Run: When the ball moves arm-side; a RHP's ball "runs" from his perspective into a RHH; synonyms "tails," "rides."

Runs Away from Arm: A pitcher who prematurely opens his hips and front side and falls off the mound, leaving his arm behind to fend for itself; this is usually a sign of poor command and may also be an injury concern depending on the severity.

Short Arm: When the arm has a noticeable bend, the arm circle is small, and the pitcher may be tense; it's also difficult to generate leverage/velocity with a shorter lever; think of a catapult.

Stiff: Lacking fluid actions and effort, can be robotic. It can often result from a pitcher with too much muscle for their body.

Sweeps: A pitch's break that is traveling more east and west than downward; a sweeping pitch usually does not have depth, but that is not always the case.

Tight: A pitch with a high spin rate; it is usually harder to see rotation, and it has a much sharper and sudden break.

Whippy, Whip: Think of a whip – long, loose, free, easy, and snaps through release; these are positives!

Wrap: The arm goes down out of the glove and back behind the pitcher's body on the downswing; it then takes an unnatural path to get back up to release that is out of alignment.

Catching Phraseology

Beats the Pitch: Has anticipation, tracks the pitch well, already has glove in position.

Catch and Throw Skills: Ability to throw out runners, have a quick transfer, throw accurately on the bag, with a strong arm.

Centers the Ball: Catches it consistently and aligns his body and glove so he isn't catching the ball off to the side of his body, which is poor presentation to get strike calls.

Comfortable: Catching can be uncomfortable to crouch all game; this player looks comfortable, and it comes naturally to them.

Does Not Obstruct: To get in the umpire's view, making it difficult for him to see strikes.

Firm Wrists: To stick a pitch and not let the velocity of the ball take the glove for a ride.

Footwork: The way the feet move, are positioned and work.

Lower Half Flexibility: Catchers that can maintain lower half flexibility are usually more athletic, and comfortable in their stance as opposed to their stiffer counterparts.

On the Bag: The ideal location and accuracy of a throw.

Pop Time: From the moment the pitch hits the catcher's mitt to the moment it hits the 2B glove or arrives at the bag. It's important to anticipate the pop of each glove.

Quiet: Not a lot of movement while catching the baseball.

Receives: The manner that the catcher catches the ball.

Set Up: How the catcher generally positions his body prior to the pitch, sometimes in relation to home plate.

Soft: Where the ball disappears into the glove, it's graceful, not stabbing, no sudden movements, easy, no violence.

Transfer: The manner in which the catcher takes the received pitch out of the glove and into the throwing hand – usually in reference to throwing out an attempted base runner.

Chapter 3

Evaluating A Player

When a high school baseball player knows scouts are watching, it's a dynamic combination of excitement and nerves. A shot at playing in the Major Leagues or landing a college scholarship is thrilling. It could be a total game-changer, not just for the player, but for their family too – it's rocket fuel for their drive to make that dream a reality. But let's be real; the pressure to nail every play can be intense.

The thought of one bad game tanking a player's chances of getting scouted can feel like an anchor. Look, scouts get the pressure and emotions players face when they're under the microscope. They know players have off days, and they don't focus on how a player does in a single game, camp, or tryout. Scouts look at consistency, growth, and how players bounce back from setbacks. They're looking at mechanics, athleticism, and mental game. So instead of obsessing over a bad game, learn from it. Grow and show scouts that you're resilient and hungry for success.

Scouts are pros at spotting potential and talent, even when players aren't at their best, considering many factors, like a player's growth potential, adaptability, and how they deal with tough times.

Even though it's normal to feel butterflies during evaluations, remember that scouts get it and are trained to see the whole picture. They know the road to success isn't always smooth, and evaluations reflect more than one game.

The 20-80 Grading System

Scouts use an industry-standard method to quantify a player's tools, known as the 20-80 scale. Like grading scales in school (A, B, C, D, F), scouting uses the 20-80 scale to consistently evaluate a player's abilities.

The 20-80 scale is often credited to Branch Rickey, although its origins remain uncertain. The scale is pretty straightforward: 50 means you're at Major League average, and you move one standard deviation for every 10 points added or subtracted. So, getting a 20 or 80? That's pretty rare.

The key to evaluating a prospect's tools is understanding what is considered average. Once you have that baseline, it's all about determining how much better or worse a player's skills are. It's easier to spot average grades in foot speed and velocities because you can measure those metrics with stopwatches and radar devices.

To illustrate the 20-80 scale and what the numbers mean, I've included a table of a general overview of the 20-80 scale, its projected frequency based on a normal distribution, and the corresponding terms for each grade:

Grade	Freq.	Rating	Description
20	0.2%	Poor	This grade is extremely rare and typically assigned to players with significant deficiencies in a specific skill or tool.
30	2.1%	Well Below Average	This grade is assigned to players who are significantly below average in a particular skill or tool.
40	13.6%	Below Average	A grade of 40 is given to players with slightly below-average abilities in a specific area.
50	68.2%	Average	This grade represents Major League average and is the benchmark for evaluating a player's tools.
60	13.6%	Plus	A grade of 60 is assigned to players who demonstrate above-average abilities in a specific skill or tool.
70	2.1%	Plus Plus	This grade is given to players who are significantly above average in a particular area, often indicating standout performance.
80	0.2%	Top End	An extremely rare grade, 80 is assigned to players with exceptional skills or tools that place them among the best in the game.

Since many players fall around "average," some organizations use the second digit (i.e., 45 or 55) to provide a more detailed breakdown in the 20-80 scale, adding the following levels:

45 – Below Average aka "Fringe Average"

50 – Average

55 – Above Average aka "Solid Average"

The 20-80 scale enables scouts to consistently evaluate and compare players based on their abilities and potential performance in the Major League.

Let me clear something up: "Major League" average is a term people often get twisted. When I'm sizing up an amateur player, I'm not comparing them to their teammates or other high school players. If I were, they'd probably be "above average" or "plus" if I'm taking the time to check them out.

Nope, I'm always judging a player against Major League Baseball players. This way, I can figure out a player's potential performance at the top level of pro baseball while keeping my evaluations of different players and age groups on point.

There's no replacing experience when mastering the 20-80 scale. When I started scouting, I had to "calibrate" my senses by watching games and learning from other scouts. For example, I wouldn't give an outfielder's arm a "60" based only on what I see from using a radar gun. I need to watch the flight path, trajectory, carry, speed, accuracy, and even how the ball bounces off the ground. A rookie scout might see a player throw at a workout (or showcase) and ask the scout next to them, "You got a 50 on that?" He'd get stared at and ignored if he did it like that (so don't), but this type of discussion helps new scouts sync up and ensure standardized and consistent evaluations.

Over time, I've learned to trust my gut and my evaluations. I can't let other people's opinions, scout talk, or evaluations mess with my head. I have faith in my evaluations and block out the noise from other scouts around me.

The 2-8 Scale – Fringe – Solid-average

Some Major League teams use a 2-8 scale instead of the 20-80. A "3" on this scale means "30," and the values essentially convey the same information as the 20-80. The reason organizations go with the 2-8 scale is to encourage their scouts to be more definitive in their grading and avoid using numbers like "45" and "65," for example. Some scouts may struggle to make a decision, notice inconsistencies in a player's performance that they want to be reflected in their rating, or they are just afraid of being wrong, so they will often say 55 or 65 or "fringe," etc.

When I was with the Minnesota Twins, they were big on using the 2-8 scale for evaluating players. The Twins GM Terry Ryan and the late Mike Radcliff would say, "Just make the call" – a player is either a 4 or 5. I remember Deron Johnson, the Twins scouting director, being super clear when he told me, "Don't ever come to me with a half!" So, even if I thought a player had slightly above-average arm or power, like a 55, there's no way I'm putting that in my scouting report. It was either a 4, 5, or 6. They wanted us to make a decision and stick to it.

The Five Tools

You've probably heard the term "Five-Tool Player" thrown around in baseball circles. A five-tool player is someone who excels in five key areas of the game: hitting for average, hitting for power, speed, fielding, and throwing. Being exceptional in all five areas is rare, but that doesn't mean you shouldn't strive to be a well-rounded athlete. If a player can demonstrate strength in all these areas, they'll likely catch the attention of scouts.

Scouts refer to the "Five Tools" when evaluating a player's potential. These are the essential skills that contribute to success on the field. Here's a rundown of the five tools and what scouts look for in each:

Tool 1: Hitting for Average

One of the most difficult evaluations scouts have to make is whether a player will be able to hit as they progress through the levels of the game. While certain factors can contribute to a player's hitting ability, such as strength, pitch recognition, and bat speed, hitting is a skill that can't be graded against Major League players. Each organization may have its own philosophy on how to grade present hitting based on a combination of factors, including a player's approach, swing plane, bat speed, strength, and results.

To properly evaluate a hitter, a scout should view them from behind home plate, their back side, and on their open side. From behind the plate, a scout can observe a hitter's stride direction, swing plane, plate coverage, and point of contact. From the open side, a scout can see a hitter's hands start, balance in their mechanics, bat speed, and bat path.

While good hitters can have all types of approaches to hitting, the most important factor is their readiness to swing and their balance with their front foot on the ground. Hall of Famer Eddie Matthews once said, "A good hitter may not be able to analyze their own swing, but they know how to swing at the right time." The ability to hit is a complex and nuanced skill, and it requires a keen eye and experience to evaluate a player's potential in this area properly.

Scouts assess a player's ability to make consistent contact with the ball and maintain a high batting average. They examine the swing mechanics, pitch recognition, and plate discipline to determine the potential for success at the plate.

Tool 2: Hitting for Power

Power is the ability to drive the ball with force, resulting in extra-base hits and home runs. Scouts look for bat speed, strength, and the ability to generate leverage in a hitter's swing. Remember, true power hitters can drive the ball to all fields, not just pull it.

Scouts have the challenging task of identifying players who have the potential to hit for power. While factors like composite bats, small ballparks, or weaker pitching can sometimes misrepresent power, scouts can assess a player's power potential in two ways: raw power and game power.

Raw power is being able to hit balls over the fence, especially in batting practice. Young players with size and physical strength often show some raw power. However, game power is what matters; it's the power that can be translated into actual numbers of home runs in a Major League season.

When evaluating power potential, scouts look for hitters who can drive the ball to all fields, not just large-framed hitters with slow bats or long swings. It's important to remember that hitting for power requires more than physical strength; it also requires proper technique and consistent solid contact in game situations.

Grading Hitters

Grading hitters is one of the most challenging tasks scouts face. The inability to adjust and maintain hitting success is often why players don't advance in baseball.

Assigning a present grade to hitting and power is difficult, especially for young prospects. Many are still physically maturing, and as scouts, we focus on their potential.

Grading the Hit Tool

It's unfair to judge a young hitter's present hit tool grade as anything higher than a "20." Many players never advance through the entire MiLB system, usually due to their inability to adjust and hit. If you placed a young, amateur player in the MLB tomorrow facing MLB pitching, they would likely struggle (20). Although the standard approach is to grade a player's current hitting as 20, in this instance, my philosophy is to grade the player against their peers, using swing mechanics as an indicator of their present hit grade.

Grading raw power vs. power performance

Many prospects don't yet possess the strength of grown men in MLB. The primary question here is, "Who will have power in the future?" The present grade of power is a combination of raw power and strength in the swing.

Determining raw power isn't an exact science. It doesn't involve a specific range of home runs a player will hit in a game situation. Instead, it's better defined as an indicator that a player has the strength and technique to hit home runs in a controlled setting, such as batting practice.

BATTERS			
Grade	Hitting (Projected Batting Average)	Power Performance (Projected Home runs)	Raw Power
80	.315+	35+	Long homers all fields
70	.295-.314	28-34	Long homers
60	.275-.294	20-27	Pull power-no doubters
50	.255-.274	14-19	Over the fence power
40	.235-.254	8-13	Gap power - fence power
30	.215-.234	4-7	Outfield power
20	.214 below	0-3	Infield power - line drives

It's important again to note the consistency of verbiage. We don't scout players by saying they will be "studs" or "big leaguers." We specify what role that player will have and what kind of performance we can expect from them.

The grade for a player's future hit tool is based on a pre-defined range of projected batting averages. It makes no sense to say a player has a Future Hit Grade of 40 and that you think he has a chance to hit in the 3-hole and hit .290.

Scouts are interested in more than home run hitters.

Power hitting is undoubtedly impressive, but it's not the only thing scouts look for in a hitter. They also value players with a solid approach at the plate, consistent contact, and the ability to drive the ball to all fields. Develop a well-rounded offensive game, and you'll increase your chances of catching a scout's eye, even if you're not hitting towering home runs every at-bat.

Here are a few other things we pay attention to:

Contact — Scouts want to see hitters who can make consistent contact and maintain a high batting average. They'll evaluate a hitter's swing mechanics, pitch recognition, and plate discipline to determine the potential for success at the plate.

Plate Discipline — Plate discipline involves a hitter's ability to recognize and lay off pitches outside the strike zone. Scouts will look for players who demonstrate strong pitch recognition, which can lead to better on-base percentages and more favorable hitting counts.

Stiffness — In an amateur player, it is important to identify stiffness. Players typically don't become more flexible and looser as they get older. Also, as they add muscle and strength, they tend to get more stiff. Stiffness lacks whip, and stiffness lacks adjustability. We want loose, adjustable swings. Can players become big leaguers with stiff swings? Absolutely. Especially if they understand their flaws and work hard to fix them. But stiffness is usually a negative marker and something we want to identify.

Hitch The most pronounced and noticeable trait in a swing is the hitch because it creates an additional move the hitter must make to get their barrel into a position to hit. This complicates the swing, and it can be exposed by velocity.

A hitter can get away with a hitch if they have tremendous pitch recognition and bat speed and make early decisions during the flight of the ball to the plate.

David Ortiz is a notable player who had a hitch in his swing. A player may have a hitch for many reasons, mainly because they feel it gives them rhythm. A hitch carries a risk because it can be difficult to break for some players. Ortiz was signed out of the Dominican Republic by Gordon Blakeley, who was then with the Seattle Mariners. Gordon recounted Ortiz's tryout and noted that he didn't hit one ball fair in batting practice, instead pulling every ball far down the line but foul. Predicting Ortiz to be a Major League hitter is a true example of scouting.

Some scouts love simplicity in swings. And they get turned off by "too many moving parts," aka the leg kick, hitch, etc. Other scouts love athletic swings with rhythm and freedom. Consider a left-handed player with a leg kick and a hitch – he has three notable traits similar to David Ortiz. However, the similarities may or may not stop there.

Tool 3: Speed

Speed is a critical tool for base running and fielding. Scouts evaluate your acceleration, top speed, and base running instincts to gauge your potential impact on the base paths and in the field.

One of the most used indicators is the time it takes a player to run from home plate to first base. However, scouts also pay attention to the player's ability to cover ground in the outfield and their speed on the base paths. If you're wondering what the stopwatches are for, this is a big one.

It's important to note that a player's usable speed may differ based on their future position or role in the game. Additionally, a player's speed may deteriorate over time, which is why scouts evaluate a player's present speed grade as the future grade.

While speed is not a tool that often improves, some players may see improvements through changes in their running form, strength training, or running programs. Players with above-average speed should aim to showcase it to scouts to maximize their potential opportunities.

Grading Speed

My stopwatch tells me what raw grade to put on a present running speed. It's really that simple. It doesn't matter if the player is 12 years old; his running time is his grade. And if that happens to be a 70 or an 80, then it is what it is. But some factors dictate the time, such as his follow-through or where he makes contact.

It's my job to determine if improved running technique or physical maturity will aid in making this runner faster in the future.

SPEED			
Grade	60 Yard Dash	Right Hand Hitter	Left Hand Hitter
80	6.4 or lower	4	3.9
70	6.5 to 6.6	4.1	4
60	6.7 to 6.8	4.2	4.1
50	6.9 to 7.0	4.3	4.2
40	7.1 to 7.2	4.4	4.3
30	7.3 to 7.4	4.5	4.4
20	7.5 and up	4.6	4.5

A lot of people don't understand that when measuring speed in baseball, a stopwatch can only provide some objective numbers, like home-to-first times, first-to-third, off the bat, and 10-40-60-yard dash lengths. It helps the scout gauge a player's raw speed But, there's more to it than just the numbers.

Skills like base running and taking extra bases don't show up on a stopwatch.

For example, a player might have a 70 raw foot speed, but it only plays like a 30 on the field. Meaning that a player might have impressive raw speed (measured as 70 on a scale with 80 being the highest) when you look at their objective measurements, like sprint times. However, when you watch them play on the field, their actual performance doesn't live up to that raw speed. In this case, it's like their speed is only playing at a 30 level, which is much lower than their potential.

This could be due to factors like poor base running instincts, slow reaction times, or the inability to use their raw speed effectively in game situations.

So, you can't rely solely on the stopwatch for the full picture. You've got to watch the players in action to understand how their speed really translates to the game. That's where the art of scouting truly shines.

Tool 4: Arm Strength

A strong arm is essential for making accurate, powerful throws from the field. Scouts assess throwing mechanics, arm strength, and accuracy to determine defensive potential.

Although the importance of arm strength may vary between positions, the ability of a shortstop to make the throw from the hole, a catcher to throw out a base-stealer, or an outfielder to cut down a run at the plate are still crucial aspects of the game. Players with good throwing mechanics are more likely to improve, as they have better control over their throws and can maximize the velocity of their throws by having their feet in the right position. Accuracy is also important, and small adjustments can improve it.

Average throws should have enough carry to reach the target and be on-line with minimal hump. A player's throwing mechanics should be evaluated based on how they position themselves to throw, the release, quickness, and body control. Players who throw with effort have a limited chance of improvement and may require better mechanics, long toss, and throwing drills.

Tool 5: Fielding

Fielding involves the ability to make plays on defense, whether it's tracking down fly balls or fielding grounders. Scouts evaluate a player's instincts, footwork, glove work, and range to determine their ability to contribute defensively.

Overall defensive skills can carry a player to the Major Leagues, especially if they play a premium position: catcher, shortstop, or centerfield. A good defensive player can also buy himself more at-bats and a chance to prove himself as a big-league hitter if he gets called up.

Along with agility and instincts, a good defensive player has a strong arm and makes accurate throws. This is especially important for outfielders who need to throw out baserunners or prevent them from advancing. Catchers also need a strong arm to throw out potential base stealers. But arm strength alone is not enough; it has to be accompanied by accuracy and timing.

Another aspect of good defense is positioning. Players who have a good understanding of the game and can anticipate where the ball is likely to be hit will put themselves in the best position to make the play. This can make up for any deficiencies in speed or arm strength.

A player's attitude and work ethic are significant factors in their defensive ability. Players willing to put in the time and effort to improve their skills and are committed to their craft are more likely to become good defensive players.

Can you improve the physical tools?

The tools a player possesses can be improved to some extent, but natural gifts like speed, power, or the ability to spin a breaking ball can set certain players apart from the rest. Recognizing and understanding one's innate abilities and limitations is crucial in determining how to enhance their skill set.

It's true that some players might have a natural talent for hitting or spinning a breaking ball, while others might need to work harder to develop those skills. But even with natural talent, there's always room for improvement. A player can refine their pitch recognition, balance, rhythm, and swing by focusing on the right training.

While certain aspects of a player's skill set can be developed through dedicated practice and training, some things are simply innate. Some players possess natural separators that distinguish them from others, making them more attractive to scouts and coaches. A player's understanding of who they are, what their role is, and what they bring to the table is incredibly valuable.

When I scout for players, I look for individuals who have a clear understanding of their strengths and weaknesses, as well as a strong desire to be the best version of themselves. By embracing their unique talents and working diligently to improve upon them, these players maximize their potential and become invaluable assets to their teams.

Don't be discouraged if natural power or speed isn't there. You can improve your skills and become a valuable player with hard work and dedication.

Mental Tools

While the Five Tools are critical, they only scratch the surface of what scouts are looking for in a player.

Scouts also evaluate things like instincts and role profiles, which give them a deeper understanding of why a player will be valuable in the long run. They're also looking at intangibles like work ethic, pregame & postgame routines, and how a player interacts with their teammates and fans. These factors combine to paint a complete picture of a player and determine their ultimate value.

The easiest part of scouting is evaluating the five tools – anyone can measure a player's speed or throwing velocity. But the real challenge is evaluating the stuff in between. Does the player have the instincts to play shortstop or centerfield? What's their first step like? These details make a difference.

Baseball IQ: Its Importance and Impact on the Game

Being a top prospect is about more than just skill and talent. Baseball IQ involves a player's knowledge of the game, situational awareness, and ability to adapt and make smart decisions on the field.

Key indicators of High Baseball IQs:

Anticipating Plays: High baseball IQ players can predict what's likely to happen next, allowing them to react quickly and make the right play in any situation.

Adjusting on the Fly: Baseball requires constant adjustments. Players with strong baseball IQs can modify their approach at the plate or in the field depending on the game situation, opponent tendencies, and their own strengths and weaknesses.

Leadership and Teamwork: Players with high baseball IQ often possess strong leadership qualities and work well with teammates. Scouts value players who communicate effectively, support teammates, and contribute to a positive team environment.

Situational Hitting: Scouts look for players who can adapt their approach at the plate based on the game situation. To excel, study different scenarios and develop a game plan for each, whether advancing a runner with a well-placed ground ball or drawing a walk in high-pressure situations.

Base Running: Smart base running creates scoring opportunities and puts pressure on the defense. Players who can read pitchers, take aggressive leads, and make wise decisions on the basepaths are what scouts are looking for. To improve, pay close attention to the game's nuances and anticipate the defense's actions.

Defensive Positioning: Understanding defensive positioning is crucial. Scouts want players who position themselves effectively based on the hitter, pitch selection, and game situation. To improve, study opposing hitters' tendencies and adjust your positioning accordingly.

Pitch Selection and Sequencing (for pitchers): High baseball IQ pitchers can effectively mix pitches and keep hitters off balance. Scouts look for pitchers who identify weaknesses in hitters and exploit them with pitch repertoire. To excel, understand the strengths and weaknesses of your pitches and adapt your approach based on the situation and hitter.

Of course, scouts look for players with the tools to succeed, whether raw power, speed, or a strong arm. But those tools are just the beginning. How they use those tools in games is what matters. A player may have a high grade for his raw power – constantly hitting towering home runs in batting practice. But they must be able to translate that into an actual playable skill in games.

Chapter 4

Importance of Athletic Markers

Athletic markers are a key part of the evaluation process. These markers are identifiable through subjective and objective measures, and they help scouts predict or project what a future athlete is going to be. It's all about identifying players who have the necessary athleticism to succeed at the highest level.

During an evaluation, I look for things like body control, change of direction, and explosive movement because these traits separate elite athletes from the rest of the pack. I want to see how well a player moves and whether they have the athleticism to succeed on the field.

Athleticism is critical in baseball because it determines a player's role on the team. While playing in the big leagues with below-average athleticism is possible, it's extremely difficult to have a significant role without it.

So, we pay close attention to athletic markers and use performances and metrics from combines to either identify players who have the potential to show athleticism in a game situation or validate any athletic markers we may have seen during a game.

Athleticism is only part of the equation. Brain function and cognition are also critical components of a player's success. A player may exhibit standout athleticism but lack the recognition or cognitive ability to react quickly enough in a game situation to utilize their skills. For example, a player may have standout speed metrics at a combine performance but lack the ability to detect a ball's trajectory off the bat to get the proper jump on it.

Let's check out some examples of combine testing.

Combine Testing

A player does not have to be fast to be considered athletic. Casual observers tend to focus on speed as a primary athletic marker. Focusing on the lower half is a great starting point, but strength and body control can also be indicative of a great athlete who may not be "fast."

Below are some examples of combine testing and athletic testing and what they are looking to measure:

10-yard dash: Quick first step, acceleration, short-range burst, base running jumps, how fast a player gets to top speed.

30-yard dash: 30 yards is 90 feet, so it purports to be an exact translation to baseball, but we have found that a 40 is a better indicator.

40-yard dash: Most applicable to baseball game situations. By the time a player rounds a bag out of the box, runs through a bag, or takes a lead (and a secondary) and begins to go first to third, we feel a player usually runs closer to 40 yards than 30 yards in a game. And it's a time that is popular in other combine testing, allowing us to standardize or use this time to identify players in football, for example.

60-yard dash: How long a player can maintain top speed.

Pro Agility: Body control, change of direction, short explosiveness.

Broad Jump, Vertical Jump: Explosiveness, lower half life.

Bat Sensor / Accelerometer (i.e., Blast Motion): Connectivity, body control with the bat, upper half explosiveness, strength.

Med Ball Toss: Body control, explosiveness, strength.

Identifying Athletic Markers Using Game Situations

Combine environments help, but a good scout can see everything he needs to during a game: body control, first-step quickness, home-to-first times, acceleration, jumps on balls, fluidity, core strength, and more.

Body control is simple and complex in its explanation – body control is how well a player's limbs, upper half, lower half, and torso work together fluidly.

You can see body control on a player that comes in hard on a slow roller/ground ball. Everything the player is doing athletically should be fluid, balanced, in sync, graceful, and controlled.

To identify body control:

- Is it fluid?

- Does it look out of sync?

- Are arms and legs flying around all over the place?

- Is the player balanced and under control?

- Does it look pretty to watch?

- Is the head moving a lot?

A player can have raw tools and poor body control, which is why scouts can't rely strictly on data. Data may show big arm strength, high exit velocity numbers, and great running times, but this does not tell the story of body control and projection.

A player can be fast and non-athletic. Conversely, a player can be a good athlete AND not run well.

If a player does not display body control, he has little chance to stay up the middle at a premium position like catcher, shortstop, or centerfield throughout his career.

A scout will find guys with better strength and agility for those positions. Body control and athletic markers are crucial for determining a player's long-term value.

Here are some key moments during a game that allow me to see athletic markers:

Situation	What It Tells Me
Pitcher's head violence	Body control, core strength, is he strong enough to do what his body is asking him to do?
Slow roller ground ball	Body control, fluidity
OF catching a ball	If you see a ball off the bat that you automatically think, "That's a hit," and it ends up getting caught in the OF, chances are that OF took a good first step toward it.
Runner takes a lead	First step quickness, watch his jumps.
Catcher blocking	Is he quick? Slow and sluggish? Active lower half? Body control?
3B fielding a groundball and turning	Is it fluid? Feet underneath him? Body control?
Hitting	Is hitter in sync? Does he stay connected, head still?
How fast does a batter get out of the box?	Not necessarily his home to first time, but how quickly can he accelerate and hit his top speed. Watch him when he starts running.
How fast does he go from 1st to 3rd?	How long does a runner take to hit his top speed? Does it happen in 10 steps? 40 steps?

Importance of brain function & cognition with respect to athleticism

As we all know, the brain and the body are connected. But when it comes to baseball, we continue to minimize the importance of cognition and the brain's role in athleticism.

A player may "look the part" and show all the signs of a premium athlete. But if his brain isn't "firing" in game situations, and he takes too long to process information, the value of his athleticism diminishes quickly. Consider the following examples of players:

- Has tremendous first-step quickness and explosiveness in the OF but struggles to identify balls off the bat.

- Has premium strength, body control, and raw power in BP but struggles to identify the spin and rotation of incoming curveballs in a game.

- Has tremendous athleticism and speed but struggles to identify a pitcher's pickoff moves and is slow to react.

These are only a few examples of how athletic markers correlate directly with cognitive ability. They explain why a player with a great 40 or 60 time isn't a lock to steal bases and why premium athletes with raw tools may have unsuccessful careers.

Brain function can be identified in a game situation, and emerging tech companies claim to be able to test these cognitive abilities and reactions in players. We should monitor these technological advances as they could aid us in the evaluation process – as a 60-yard dash does. Meaning these pieces of tech could validate what we see with our eyes during a game.

Chapter 5

Scouting by Position – Can They Play?

When I started scouting, it was easy to get lost in tools, grades, and raw athleticism.

But today, even with the ease of gathering exit velocities, spin rates, 60 times, and other metrics, a seasoned veteran scout understands that there is much more to the game of baseball.

Although some amateur scouts, scouting services, social media scouts, and others drool over player measurables, I can't let myself get lost in the numbers.

I can analyze tools. I can analyze swings. I can put grades on guys. I can look for stiffness. I can identify baseball athleticism. But I don't ever lose the forest through the trees.

Because after everything is said and done, the question I have to ask myself is … Can they play?

I constantly look for players who produce in games and show the desired markers. I want to see body control, baseball athleticism, instincts, and in-game production. Tools are an important piece of the puzzle, but a player will have a hard time advancing in baseball if he cannot apply those tools in games.

After evaluating a player's tools, I can better determine their role by watching their in-game action.

Describing how many games, at-bats, or innings I have seen a player play is a critical part of a written scouting report. My opinion and evaluation become more accurate, respected, and valid the more times I get to watch a player.

If I'm submitting a report for a player I saw at only one game, it may have been his best or worst day.

The more games I go to, the better my chance of seeing the "real" player I'm looking for.

The Value of Tools by Position

Over the years, the tools scouts look for in specific positions have changed, and the way an organization values tools can vary from club to club.

Hitting has always been a premium tool. In the 1960s, pitching dominated baseball, elevating defense at positions up the middle of the field in the hierarchy of tools. Today, good hitters are found at traditionally weaker hitting positions of the past.

The following list provides a general hierarchy of tools most desired for each position and is referred to as *player profiling by position.*

Position	Order of Tool Value				
Catcher	Fielding	Hitting	Arm	Power	Speed
1st Base	Hitting	Power	Fielding	Arm	Speed
2nd Base	Hitting	Fielding	Power	Speed	Arm
3rd Base	Hitting	Power	Fielding	Arm	Speed
Shortstop	Fielding	Arm	Hitting	Speed	Power
Left Field	Hitting	Power	Fielding	Speed	Arm
Centerfield	Hitting	Fielding	Speed	Power	Arm
Right Field	Hitting	Power	Fielding	Arm	Speed

There are a few notes to consider about the table above:

- The tools are listed in order of most important to that position in the second column to least important in the last column and represent a consensus among scouts with backgrounds from different organizations.

- This list could vary depending on an organization's needs. For example, hypothetically, the Chicago Cubs may tell their scouts that the Hit Tool is the most important tool they seek in a Shortstop. Or the Boston Red Sox may seek Power above all in their Left Fielder.

- Each tool is not equally important across positions. For example, a shortstop's power tool is in much higher demand than a catcher's speed.

- Some tools may not be listed as #1 or #2 but could be a deal-breaker for that position. For example, a club may be able to overlook that their 2nd baseman can't hit for power if he is a plus hitter and plus defender. But an organization may not be able to overlook having a centerfielder who is not a plus runner – yet both are listed third on their respective positional importance.

What Scouts Look for by Position

Outfielders

When scouts evaluate outfielders, they're searching for players who can hit for power, cover ground efficiently, track fly balls, and make strong, accurate throws.

Power Hitting: Typically, outfielders are expected to provide power at the plate. Scouts will evaluate bat speed, strength, and ability to drive the ball to all fields.

Range: Scouts assess an outfielder's ability to cover ground quickly, both laterally and forward or backward. Speed, instincts, and good routes all contribute to a player's range.

Glove Work: Scouts want to see smooth, reliable glove work when fielding fly balls and grounders. They look for players who can make catches in stride and transfer the ball to their throwing hand quickly and efficiently.

Arm Strength and Accuracy: An outfielder's ability to make strong, accurate throws can be a game-changer. Scouts evaluate throwing mechanics, arm strength, and accuracy to determine a player's potential impact on defense.

Centerfield

••

Centerfield is often seen as a position for high-speed players, but many average runners also play centerfield. A lot of this depends on how a team is constructed. It's crucial for a centerfielder to get good breaks, avoid false steps, and not let the ball get behind them. Think of centerfielders like shortstops – they need that internal compass, the ability to move in all directions, keep balls in front of them, and direct traffic.

A centerfielder should have enough ground coverage to catch balls that go up to a certain height. Different types of players can play centerfield, like George Springer, who sometimes plays right field if there's a faster player with similar defensive abilities available. Mookie Betts is another example of a player who could play centerfield but playing a corner is a better fit for him and the organization depending on who is in centerfield.

The position of centerfield has evolved over time, moving away from just the fastest runners to players who have sufficient speed and play instinctual defense. Jim Edmonds and Ken Griffey Jr. are great examples from different eras. Edmonds wasn't a burner, but his instincts allowed him to play a Gold Glove centerfield. Griffey Jr. was the prototypical centerfielder with his speed and ability to cover ground and make incredible plays. The game today rightfully focuses more on players who can effectively play centerfield based on instincts rather than just speed alone.

Right & Left Field

Right fielders need to be able to make strong throws to third base to prevent runners from taking that extra base. The importance of arm strength has decreased in recent years due to changes in ballparks and the game itself, but it's still vital for outfielders to deter runners from advancing.

Corner outfielders should be particularly skilled at guarding the line and preventing extra bases. They must provide enough protection to prevent runs and stop doubles or triples as much as possible.

In right field, making plays with the arm is even more crucial. Exceptional arm strength is rare, but the outfield positions need to be able to prevent runners from attempting to advance.

Middle Infielders

Middle infielders, including shortstops and second basemen, must be agile and quick-thinking to excel defensively.

Quickness and Footwork: Scouts evaluate a middle infielder's ability to move laterally, first-step quickness, and overall footwork. These attributes are essential for making plays on ground balls and turning double plays.

Soft Hands: Scouts want to see infielders with soft hands, meaning they can field grounders cleanly and make smooth transfers to their throwing hands. This skill is critical for turning double plays and minimizing errors.

Baseball IQ: Middle infielders need to be aware of game situations and make quick decisions on the field. Scouts look for players who demonstrate solid instincts and situational awareness, which can lead to better defensive play.

Good feet, a lively body, athleticism, body control, and the ability to change direction are essential for handling plays like the slow roller or making a throw from the hole between the shortstop and second base.

Middle Infielders need good hands, quick feet, and a strong understanding of how to maneuver around the bag. Spatial awareness is a must for this position. Imagine someone standing in the middle of a circle, having to move in all directions without any false steps, misreads, or unnecessary movements.

Shortstop is an instinctual position, and scouts want players who can consistently make routine plays, handle slow rollers, throw accurately from the hole, and excel around the bag at second base. They must have an internal compass that allows them to move in every direction possible while still making a play.

Making routine plays with consistency is mandatory. Many infielders can make exceptional plays because that's what they practice, but they struggle to make routine plays. Players will have more opportunities for routine plays in game situations.

Scouts prefer instinctual players over flashy, athletic players, even if they are half a step slower. A player with good instincts, spatial awareness, and the ability to direct traffic in the infield while consistently executing plays is a more valuable asset to the team.

Corner Infielders

Corner infielders, including first and third basemen, are often expected to contribute offensively and defensively.

Power Hitting: Corner infielders are typically expected to provide power at the plate. Scouts will evaluate bat speed, strength, and ability to drive the ball to all fields.

Glove Work and Range: Scouts want corner infielders who can handle their defensive responsibilities, including fielding grounders, making throws, and, for first basemen, receiving throws from other infielders. Range, glove work, and arm strength all factor into these evaluations.

Reactions and Instincts: Quick reactions and strong instincts are essential for corner infielders, who often have less time to react to batted balls. Scouts will look for players who can read the ball off the bat and make quick, decisive plays in the field.

First Base

The most crucial defensive attribute for a first baseman is their bat. That doesn't mean scouts don't want first basemen with soft hands and a good fit around the bag. However, their range needs to be limited to 5 to 6 yards in either direction, as going further would take them out of the play at the base.

A good first baseman should be skilled to their left, be able to protect the line, and take away a ball a couple of yards in the hole. They should also have an understanding of base runners, possess soft hands (good wrists) for receiving the ball, and be able to adjust accordingly. Flexibility is essential in this position – you can't be a stiff-body player. Surprisingly, even some big-bodied players like Mark McGwire, Logan Morrison, Fred McGriff, and Sid Bream could perform splits and were flexible.

Poor athletes can't play first base. Even David Ortiz, who wasn't very good around the bag due to his hands and rhythm, could still manage some flexibility. So, a first baseman must be good for a short distance and have good hands and wrists.

Third Base

Many scouts view third base as a bat-first position, but it's important to recognize that many third basemen in the league are also quite skilled defenders. Players like Kyle Seager, Justin Turner, and Alex Bregman are more than capable defensively. When you look around the league, you see players like Anthony Rendon, one of the best defenders I've personally scouted.

Third base isn't a position to be filled by just anyone; you need a player who can hit well, maintain a high batting average, hit for power, and have a low swing-miss rate. Note that I said, "low swing-miss rate," not "low strikeout rate." A good third baseman should be able to produce when needed and protect the double while making tough plays and fielding bunts.

Shortstops and second basemen are expected to cover ground left and right. So, third basemen and first basemen need to be able to cover the line effectively.

Catchers

A unique set of skills and characteristics set catchers apart from other positions on the field. Catchers manage the game, control the pitching staff, and direct traffic on the field. They must be natural leaders and quick thinkers, as they're the only ones who can see the entire field in front of them.

Catchers manage the game from behind the plate, and scouts value strong defensive skills, leadership, and game management.

Receiving and Framing: Scouts assess a catcher's ability to receive and frame pitches, which can help pitchers get called strikes. They look for smooth, quiet hands and the ability to present pitches effectively to the umpire.

Blocking and Throwing: Catchers need to be able to block pitches in the dirt and throw out base stealers. Scouts evaluate blocking technique and throwing accuracy when controlling the running game.

Catcher's pop time: People always ask about the stopwatch. Scouts measure the catcher's "pop time," which is the time it takes to receive the pitch, transfer the ball to their throwing hand, and throw it to second base. This is an essential skill for controlling the opponent's running game, and a quick pop time indicates a strong and accurate throwing arm.

One thing I need to distinguish – pop time and glove transfer metrics really only matter when they are captured in game situations.

Game Management and Leadership: Scouts will look for players to manage the game, communicate with pitchers, demonstrate strong leadership, and make smart decisions on the field.

Catchers must be able to process multiple factors instantly, such as the next hitter, ball location, game situation, inning, and more, requiring exceptional baseball intelligence and instinct.

In addition to their mental acuity, catchers need to possess excellent hands and feet to handle the demands of the position. They must receive pitches effectively, block balls in the dirt, and work seamlessly with their pitching staff. Throwing is another critical aspect of the catcher's skillset, although it's sometimes considered secondary to game management and pitch calling.

Excellent catchers are hard to find, and teams may compromise on certain aspects like pitch calling or throwing ability. Despite these compromises, a good catcher remains a highly valuable asset to a team.

Pitchers
....

When evaluating a pitcher, I prioritize my assessment process. First, I focus on the pitcher's success against hitters, considering their stuff, life, swings and misses, explosiveness, and plate life. Next, I evaluate their body, arm action, and other projection markers.

For amateur players, I've noticed swings and misses become less important as they get older. High school pitching prospects usually dominate their peers, regardless of their physical appearance.

I've seen pitchers come in various shapes and sizes, from Bartolo Colon to Billy Wagner. Seeing a wide range of physicality on the mound has taught me that a less athletic player with good coordination in their delivery can still make it to the big leagues.

Although I generally prefer athletic pitchers with projection and clean, easy arms, I've learned to evaluate their stuff first. I don't dismiss a pitcher with good stuff because their appearance on the mound is less than ideal. Pitching is a specialized skill and, in many ways, easier than hitting.

As I talked about earlier, hitting a baseball is one of the most challenging tasks in sports, requiring a special athlete and player to excel in hitting, base running, and defense. In contrast, most of a pitcher's job is complete once they release the ball, so pitchers with less athletic bodies or weaker athletic markers can make it in professional baseball. For a hitter, the release of the pitch is just the beginning of their job description, making their overall athletic ability even more critical.

Since pitchers are the focal point of the game, scouts are constantly searching for those with the right mix of velocity, control, and pitch variety. Here's what they look for:

Velocity: If you haven't figured it out already, velocity is what all those *dead-giveaway-there's-a-scout-here* radar guns are measuring. While it's not the only factor, velocity does play a significant role in a pitcher's evaluation. Scouts will assess fastball velocity and the difference in speed between fastball and off-speed pitches.

Grading the Fastball

Scouts usually evaluate a pitcher's velocity by the radar gun reading out of the hand, which requires little or no guesswork. However, the scout must evaluate the effectiveness of the pitch when entering a grade for the fastball based on its movement, life, and command/control. Scouts can use a combination of his eyes, ears, hitter's results, or even a more advanced radar/optical capturing system like Trackman to determine the effectiveness of a pitch.

Generally speaking, the following velocities correspond to the correct ballpark grade on the 20-80 scale:

Fastball Speed	
Grade	Fastball MPH
80	98+
70	96-97
60	94-95
55	93-94
50	92-93
45	91-92
40	90-91
30	88-89
20	86-87

Control and Command: Pitchers must be able to throw strikes and locate their pitches effectively. Scouts will evaluate control (throwing strikes) and command (hitting specific spots in or outside of the strike zone) to determine potential effectiveness on the mound.

Pitch Variety: Scouts want to see pitchers with a diverse arsenal of pitches that can keep hitters off-balance. They'll evaluate the quality and effectiveness of a pitcher's fastball, breaking ball, changeup, and any other pitches in their repertoire.

Pitch Effectiveness: The effectiveness of a pitch is not solely determined by its behavior, such as velocity, movement, or spin rate, but also by how hitters react to it.

Fastball Quality: A pitcher might throw a 90mph slider with 2 feet of break and a 3000 spin rate, which may appear as a 70-grade pitch during a bullpen session. However, if that pitch consistently gets hammered in games, the grade must be adjusted accordingly. Even if the pitch appears nasty, but hitters continue to hit it, I wouldn't give it a grade lower than 40 as a baseline. Evaluating a pitch's effectiveness requires considering both its inherent qualities and the real-world results it produces during games.

I always start with fastball quality when evaluating a pitcher's arsenal. Velocity is undoubtedly crucial, but many other factors contribute to fastball quality. When assessing a fastball, I consider the following:

- Is the fastball effective?
- Does it have life or movement?
- Does it feel heavy or light to the hitters?
- Can the pitcher control and command the fastball?
- Does the pitcher challenge hitters with it?
- Is the fastball delivered with ease or effort?
- Is it a 2-seam or 4-seam fastball?

All these elements combine to paint a more comprehensive picture of a pitcher's fastball quality and overall potential.

Light vs. Heavy: I will often differentiate between "light" and "heavy" fastballs when evaluating pitchers. These terms represent opposite characteristics of a fastball.

A light fastball typically has these qualities:

- Hitters can easily lift it in the air.

- Catchers can effortlessly receive it, which may not produce a noticeable pop in the mitt.

On the other hand, a heavy fastball:

- Is more difficult for hitters to lift.

- Hitters often struggle to make solid contact.

- Produces a more pronounced pop in the mitt when caught.

While it's true that scouts love to see pitchers with blazing fastballs, velocity isn't the only factor they consider. Command, pitch movement, and the ability to change speeds are equally important when evaluating a pitcher's potential. If you don't have a 90+ MPH fastball, don't despair. Focus on refining your overall pitching repertoire and demonstrating your ability to keep hitters off balance.

Intent: Many pitchers today train to increase their fastball velocity by throwing as hard as possible. While aggressiveness and the desire to improve velocity can be positive, these efforts must translate to game situations without leading to excessive strain or head violence. Ultimately, the effectiveness of a pitcher's fastball is determined by how well it performs during games and not just during practice or bullpen sessions.

Number of quality pitches: When evaluating high school pitchers, scouts understand they might only showcase two quality pitches. This doesn't necessarily mean they can't develop a third pitch; they just have more time and room for growth. At the high school level, a pitcher might dominate hitters with just a fastball, as throwing a changeup at 80 mph could match the bat speed of high school hitters.

On the other hand, when scouting college pitchers, I expect to see more refinement and development of a third pitch. College pitchers have had more time and experience to hone their skills and expand their pitch repertoire. If a college pitcher only displays two quality pitches, they're more likely suited for a reliever role. Their development path might be shorter, and they might not have the same level of potential growth as a high school pitcher. Consequently, I'll consider the level of competition and developmental stage when evaluating pitchers and projecting their future roles.

Stretch vs. Windup: Every scouting report I've ever written includes a thorough assessment of the pitcher in the stretch position. I want to ensure the velocity is maintained, the breaking pitches remain high-quality, and the pitcher doesn't experience any significant drop-off when in the stretch. Interestingly, some pitchers perform even better in the stretch.

When a pitcher excels from the stretch, it could indicate that they might be better suited for a bullpen role. Relievers often pitch from the stretch to minimize the time it takes to deliver the pitch and to maintain better control over baserunners. In contrast, starting pitchers usually use the windup, allowing them to generate more power and maintain their rhythm over a longer outing.

Ultimately, scouts must evaluate pitchers in both the stretch and windup positions to understand their abilities and project their most suitable roles in the future.

Evaluating the Off-Speed: I consider several aspects of the pitch when evaluating a breaking ball:

- The general shape of the pitch, noting whether it is 12-6, 11-5, 10-4, sweeping, or a downer.

- When the breaking action starts (late break being preferable).

- If it is detectable right out of the hand or if it has good "tunneling" and looks like a fastball until the late break occurs.

- Whether the pitch is loopy or sharp (loopy pitches are less effective because they are more easily detected).

- If the pitcher can throw it for strikes and if hitters struggle with it, whether they swing and miss, and if it serves as an out pitch or a "get-me-over" pitch.

- The pitcher's command of the pitch and if they have variations of it.

- The pitch's speed relative to the fastball.

- The pitcher's arm speed, and if they throw it from the same angle.

- If the pitcher maintains command of the pitch from the stretch and with runners on, they rely on it in certain circumstances, and if the pitch has a tight, high-spin quality.

When grading a breaking ball, a "50" grade curveball or slider is considered a quality pitch that the pitcher can throw for strikes. While big league hitters might hit it sometimes, it generally gets outs, occasionally swings and misses, and achieves average success.

A breaking ball with more bite, tighter spin, and increased swing and miss potential becomes a "60" grade breaking ball.

The key to changeups is deception. It should look like a fastball, with the same arm speed and a good speed differential of around 12mph. Late sink adds to its effectiveness.

Knuckleballs are not usually something we often see in young pitchers because that pitch is typically developed later in a player's career. Players who throw good knuckleballs often didn't enter the league with them.

Starters vs. Relievers

Pitching roles can range from starters to relievers, setup guys, closers, or even further categorized into #1 through #5 starters, short relievers, and long relievers. To determine a pitcher's role, we must look at certain indicators to help us understand their capabilities and strengths.

Generally, the more skilled a pitcher is, the more times they can effectively go through the lineup. Here are some factors to consider when evaluating a pitcher's role:

	Starters	Relievers
Stamina	Need endurance to pitch multiple innings.	Often pitch just one or two innings.
Pitch Repertoire	Usually need to have a wider variety of pitches to be effective throughout the game.	Can be successful with fewer pitch types as long as they are highly effective.
Consistency	Should demonstrate consistent performance.	May have more fluctuation in their results due to pitching limited innings.
Ability to Adjust	Must adjust their approach as they face the lineup multiple times in a game.	May only need to face the lineup once.
Mental Fortitude	Should have the mental toughness to handle the pressure of being on the mound for an extended period and recover from occasional setbacks.	Often need to be ready to step in and perform at a high level in high-pressure situations.

Considering these factors help scouts to better define a pitcher's role and understand their role the team's overall pitching strategy.

Two-Way Players

Two-way players are extremely rare in professional baseball, and very few have succeeded at a high level in pitching and hitting. Shohei Ohtani is one notable example in current baseball, as he excels in both aspects of the game and has the potential to become one of the best players ever. Another example is Brendan McKay, who was drafted by Tampa Bay in the first round and played both roles in the minor leagues. However, he has primarily been a pitcher in the big leagues.

Conversion players like Bobby Darwin and Rick Ankiel have played both roles at different times in their careers, but the list of true two-way players in professional baseball is short. Most clubs will require a player to choose one role due to the demands on the body, the focus needed, the refinement, and the mental grind.

In college, it is more common to find two-way players, usually everyday players who also serve as relievers. This can make a player more valuable to a college team if they can legitimately perform in both roles. However, for overall career development, it's not generally encouraged.

When evaluating a player who is a prospect in one role, it can be helpful to watch them perform in another role to assess their athleticism, instincts, cognitive function, and overall physical capabilities. However, it is still crucial to focus primarily on their prospective role to determine their potential in professional baseball.

Changing Positions

If a player has good speed and power but struggles to play a certain position, they may need to consider switching positions to find success.

Ultimately, you want to play a premium position until you can't defensively hang there anymore. Playing centerfield, shortstop, or catcher is essential for a player's long-term success in the game. If you can't hang defensively in one of these positions, it will be tough to stick around.

However, with the rise of analytics in baseball, some positions have become more forgiving regarding defensive positioning. For example, catcher arm strength has become increasingly less important as stolen bases have gone away.

But as the game shifts and players start using the whole field again, and with the rule changes, traditional profiles and positions will become more important. Whether they should've changed or not in the first place is a different topic altogether, but I digress.

If a player can hit, though, the team will find a spot for them. The tools will carry them, but they'll eventually get moved if they can't play defense at their current position. Some defensive skills are instinctual and innate, while others can be developed. But at the end of the day, a player must have a baseline of natural instincts, ball-reading ability, and foot quickness to succeed defensively.

My advice to any player considering a position change is to focus on improving their skills at their current position first. But if they can't succeed there, they may need to consider switching positions to find their niche in the game.

Chapter 6

Using Data Technology in Player Evaluations

With the advances in analytics and technology, scouts increasingly utilize data-driven methods to complement traditional scouting techniques. Radar tracking systems, video analysis, and advanced statistical models provide a more in-depth understanding of a player's performance and potential.

The role of data analytics in scouting will continue to improve, revealing more indicators over time. Remember that pro scouting is about the "future," and data represents the "now."

We aren't close to a point where the data can effectively project and define roles 4-8 years down the line. But most scouts with a decent understanding of data and ways to incorporate it into the evaluation process will be more dynamic evaluators, offering long-term value to the club they represent.

To make the most of today's technology, scouts should begin an evaluation with their subjective perspective and trained eyes, then understand, validate, and incorporate data into the overall process.

Let me break down the data categories scouts may consider in an evaluation:

Ball flight metrics: Use of radars and camera systems to track the ball's behavior when it leaves a pitcher's hand or a hitter's bat. Systems like Trackman, Flightscope, Hawkeye, and Rapsodo, help scouts gather this information.

Biomechanical data: Player's body movements, including weight transfer, swing sequencing, arm stress and arm path of a pitcher, and more.

Bat data: Scouts can analyze a player's bat movement using technology from companies like Blast Motion and Diamond Kinetics. By attaching accelerometers to the player's bat, they can gather data like time to impact, attack angle, approach angle, hand speed, and connectivity.

Performance data: Tracking player performance in areas such as chasing bad pitches, whiffs, solid contacts, soft contacts, pitching strategy, throwing strikes, etc.

Sabermetric or statistical data: Considers batting average, OPS, FIP, WHIP, and other advanced statistics.

Cognitive data: Examines how a player processes information and reacts, usually in a controlled environment using lights, lasers, virtual reality, or apps on an iPad.

Athletic data: Includes results from tests measuring athleticism, such as the 60-yard dash, med ball testing, pro agilities, and more.

Legacy data or classic data: Using data generated by the radar gun or stopwatch.

By understanding and utilizing these different data categories, scouts can build a comprehensive player evaluation and better project their future potential in baseball.

Sabermetrics

Sabermetrics is the analysis and study of baseball statistics and data to measure player performance and evaluate in-game strategies objectively. Baseball writer and historian Bill James coined the term "sabermetrics" from a combination of the acronym SABR (Society for American Baseball Research) and the word "metrics."

Sabermetrics involves using advanced statistical methods to analyze various aspects of the game, such as player performance, team performance, and strategic decision-making. Traditional baseball statistics like batting average, earned run average (ERA), and runs batted in (RBI) have long been used to evaluate players. However, sabermetrics aims to provide a more comprehensive and accurate understanding of a player's true value by considering additional metrics like on-base percentage (OBP), slugging percentage (SLG), wins above replacement (WAR), and many others.

Sabermetrics has gained significant popularity and acceptance in recent years, with many Major League Baseball (MLB) teams incorporating advanced analytics into their front-office decision-making processes. Using sabermetrics in player evaluation, game strategy, and roster construction has definitely changed how the game is played, analyzed, and understood.

Hitter Data – Whiff, Chase, and More

Scouts recognize the value of sabermetric data like Whiff, Chase, Solid Contact, Barrels, and Strike percentages. These data points can give a better understanding of a player's aptitude and long-term performance potential, which, in turn, can help determine whether a player is a project or already excelling.

Metrics like exit velocity, pitch velocity, break, and spin can improve over time with strength and skill development, and metrics like whiffing and chasing provide insight into a player's mental acuity. Scouts can assess pitch recognition, strike zone discipline, and overall understanding of the pitcher's strategy.

The following metrics have been tracked for a long time and may offer a glimpse into a player's hand-eye coordination.

Whiff: When a player swings at a pitch and misses. Frequent whiffs can be a red flag.

Chase: A player swinging at a pitch out of the zone for a ball, which can reveal insights into pitch recognition, plate discipline, and strike zone awareness.

Barrels: An exit velocity within 10 mph of the player's peak. For example, if player John Doe's max exit velocity is 100 mph, any ball from 90 mph to 100 mph is considered a "barrel," indicating proper hand-eye coordination and good bat-to-ball contact.

These metrics can be charted from video with trained eyes or used in spreadsheets and filtered to draw the necessary conclusions. You don't always need fancy equipment or systems to produce usable data.

Exit Velocity (EV)

Exit Velocity is a key indicator of a player's current strength and overall efficiency in their swing mechanics. In my experience, younger players who have a lot of raw power tend to have higher exit velocities. However, I've also seen that players who use their bodies and the ground well can achieve higher exit velocities even if they don't have as much raw power.

When evaluating a player's exit velocity, I confirm what I see with my eyes and hear with my ears. It's not just about the numbers on the radar gun. A player with an easy swing may have a lower exit velocity, but the ball just sounds different off the bat, indicating a potential for success. I always prioritize my core instincts; exit velocity is only one piece of the puzzle when evaluating a player's overall potential.

Max Exit Velocity (MAX EV) – This shows the CURRENT raw power that the player is capable of if it is measured during Batting Practice. Tracking it during a game will give even better insights.

Average Exit Velocity (AVG EV) – This shows how often the player squares up the ball within the range of their max power and how often they barrel it. If a player has a 100mph max EV in batting practice but only has a 75mph average EV in the game, it's not a good sign. During player development, if a player's average EV in the cage increases each week, it doesn't necessarily mean they're getting stronger; they may be getting more efficient and consistently squaring up the ball.

Pitcher Data – Spin Rate, Tilt, Movement Profiles, etc.

Pitcher metrics can be helpful to the evaluation process. Ball flight out of a pitcher's hand is becoming increasingly prevalent as a valuable evaluation tool. Radar-based systems (Trackman, Flightscope, Rapsodo) and camera-based systems (Hawk-eye, Pitch f/x) can capture spin, movement, break, velocity, and more of the ball. Listed below are a few highlights:

Spin rate: In MLB, the average fastball spin rate hovers around 2200-2300 rpm. Fastballs with spin rates in this range are generally hittable and exhibit "average" behavior. Scouts are looking for pitchers whose spin rates fall outside this zone, either abnormally high or abnormally low.

Abnormally high spin rates give the ball "life" and zip, making it more challenging for hitters. Low spin rates usually result in pitches with more sink. High-spin pitchers often try to keep their pitches up in the zone, while low-spin pitchers aim to sink their pitches down out of the zone. Understanding these spin-rate differences helps a scout better evaluate pitchers and their potential effectiveness on the mound.

Tilt: This is the direction the ball is spinning around an axis, such as side spin or backspin, and is usually represented by a clock. The hour hand is used to indicate the tilt direction. For example, a spin tilt of 1 o'clock for a right-handed pitcher (RHP) is "up" and to the "right," resulting in the ball tailing or running to the right. Here are some examples of tilt and the resulting pitch movement:

- RHP fastball at 11 o'clock: Cutter or cutting action

- Pitch at 6 o'clock: Straight downward 12-6 curveball break

- RHP pitch at 9 o'clock: Gyro or frisbee slider

- RHP pitch at 3 o'clock: Changeup or sidearm pitcher with run to the right

- Spin tilt directly dictates the way the ball will break; a ball can't spin left and break right.

A pitcher with an average spin rate of 2200-2300 rpm and a tilt at 12:15 is throwing a very hittable (average) spin rate, with almost straight backspin (12:15), likely with very little horizontal movement and not high enough spin to challenge the hitter. A pitcher with a 2500-2600 rpm spin rate and a fastball tilt of 1:45 is a high spin guy, likely producing some sharp arm-side run (in on a right-handed hitter).

Movement profiles: Scouts analyze movement profiles, which are combinations of horizontal and vertical movement that provide the exact break of each pitch. For instance, a right-handed pitcher (RHP) with a curveball that has -8 inches of vertical break (dropping 8 inches) and -2 inches of horizontal break (breaking left from their perspective by 2 inches) offers insight into the pitch's shape. A RHP throwing a breaking ball with -2 inches of vertical break and -8 inches of horizontal break might call that pitch a "curveball," but it has more slider-like (east to west) action with minimal vertical or downward break.

Despite the movement data, a pitch's effectiveness depends on how batters perform against it. A pitch with impressive spin, break, and movement might still be ineffective if batters consistently hit it well. The scout's job is to consider all these factors when evaluating a pitcher's potential.

Here's a breakdown of Fastball and Curveball Spin rates and what they represent:

Fastballs	
2600+	Elite / High Spin
2400-2600	Well Above Average
2200-2400	Average
2000-2200	Below Average
1800-2000	Sinking Action / Low Spin
Curveballs	
2900+	Elite Spin
2700-2900	Above Average
2500-2700	Average
2300-2500	Below Average
2100-2300	Well Below Average
1900-2100	Poor

Sliders are fairly similar to curveballs in terms of spin rate. Changeups typically have spin rates below 2000 rpm and often tumble out of the hand in the 1500 rpm range. Knuckleballs can have spin rates in the hundreds of rpm, but they are often misread by tracking systems.

Cutters usually have a higher spin rate than fastballs by a couple hundred rpm. For example, if you see a right-handed pitcher with an 11:00 tilt on the fastball and a 2700 rpm spin rate, he's most likely throwing cutters. This is because the spin rate is higher, and the tilt indicates cutting rather than running action. As a scout, it's crucial to understand these nuances to evaluate a pitcher's repertoire and potential accurately.

PITCHF/x

PITCHF/x was the first system to track pitch movement and is still used today. Using camera vision, PITCHF/x tracks the break and movement of a pitch along a 9-point trajectory during its flight to the plate. This technology is most commonly used to determine the horizontal and vertical break of a pitch.

Over the years, PITCHF/x has been instrumental in building a vast database of pitch movement data. Other technologies, like Trackman, have since emerged that utilize radar and a much higher sample rate (thousands of times during the ball flight) to provide even more accurate data.

To maintain the legacy of the PITCHF/x database and years of data, newer technologies like Trackman, and Flightscope also provide additional data in a PITCHF/x -friendly format.

Movement profiles have become a critical part of evaluating and developing pitches. To give you an idea, here is a sample chart of a player's arsenal:

Pitch	Vertical Break	Horizontal Break	Comment
FB	3.55	9.13	Running fastball (moving "right" from pitcher's perspective) getting a lot of horizontal break/run in on a RHH. This player may throw from a 3/4 or lower slot to produce this type of H movement, and you should likely see spin tilts in the 1:30-3:00 range to reflect that.
CB	-12.44	-1.09	This is a hard breaking, downer curveball. You should expect to see a tilt in the 6:00 to 7:00 range. Any tilt creeping towards 9:00 would have produced more horizontal "sweeping" motion and less vertical break. (It would be considered more slider than curveball in that case)
SL	0.41	-10.98	This is a sweeping slider with very little downward depth and a lot of horizontal movement that's staying on the same pitch plane.
CH	1.09	0.98	This is a straight change that is getting no movement, no sink, no run. It is likely an ineffective pitch in its current state, but we always try to use our eyes and other information to see if it's deceptive in other ways (good tunneling, quality arm speed, excellent location, good change of speed) and resulting in swings and misses.

You rarely see breaks approaching 15-20 inches in any direction. Without getting into too much detail here, anything in the double digits usually gets a lot of break.

Fastballs have positive vertical break. The ball has backspin and is fighting gravity. It is not necessarily moving "up," but staying truer "straight" and not getting a downward angle. This is why this is considered a pitch that has "late life," or "late giddy up," or "explodes," or "throws a heavy ball." If a guy has a lot of positive vertical break on the fastball and a high spin rate, it explains why he is so effective with that pitch at the top of the zone. The pitch stays "up," and the hitter struggles to match the plane with the barrel. If that pitch is thrown at the bottom of the zone, it will stay straight, and the hitter has a better chance.

Chapter 7

Projecting a Player's Future Potential

I'm often asked, "Why isn't my kid being scouted? He's a much better player than another kid on his team who is getting a lot of interest from scouts."

Remember, pro scouting is never about the *now*. It is always about the *future*.

Projection is the art and science of looking into the future and trying to predict what a player will become. Many parents misunderstand this concept. One high school player may far outperform another when looking at stats, but their potential for improvement may not match.

If that's the case, your player may be more successful in catching the attention of college coaches.

College baseball places a strong emphasis on the present because college coaches have a limited window to achieve success. If they don't win, they lose their jobs. Major league organizations have a minor league system, where managers and general managers can spend several years building a team before seeing results. College programs must recruit players who can step in and win games immediately.

Athletic recruiting in the college realm is different from professional scouting. College coaches don't consider themselves scouts; they are recruiters, and scouting is a term reserved for the professional sphere.

A late bloomer may not receive much attention from college recruiters but could thrive under the guidance of professional scouts who recognize their potential to develop and grow.

Consider a player who doesn't stand out in high school but gradually improves in college. He may not be a star recruit, but his instincts and future abilities could make him a valuable asset in the major leagues. Good professional scouting involves identifying the potential for growth and evolution, as players typically don't reach their full potential until their mid-20s or later.

Rankings and evaluations focusing on present-day performance often fail to predict future success because they don't account for the growth and development that can happen in the years following high school and college.

When it comes to picking future stars, scouting is all about envisioning a player's potential. Scouts call this "dreaming." Anyone can report the facts when they see a guy throw a 92-mph fastball. But the real challenge is figuring out why that 92-mph pitch plays like it's 97 or predicting a batter's future game power. Projecting a hitter's ability to make consistent contact is tough, and no matter how many analytics you throw at it, you can't be certain if a guy will be a great hitter unless you watch him over and over again. That's what makes scouting such a fascinating and complex job.

One nugget I picked up from MLB veteran scout Stan Meek when visiting one day involved what worked and what didn't. We discussed process, and when we mentioned one's experience evaluating players, he replied, "Well, the more you see, the faster you understand what you're looking for."

Projection is not only based on career trajectory—everyone projects. It's just a matter of how.

There are different types of projection, such as mental, role, skill, and tool. Scouts consider all these factors and more when projecting what a player will become.

To make an accurate projection, scouts must analyze where a player is on their trajectory in life. Is he a 14-year-old with plenty of time to grow and develop? Is he 23 and approaching his peak? Was he an early bloomer or a late developer with untapped potential?

Age is a factor in projection, but it's not the only one. For example, Tim Tebow and Michael Jordan entered the Minor League system much older than traditional prospects. Yet, they still had projection because of their unique backgrounds and athletic abilities.

Present strength and physicality may not fit the "ideal" prospect mold, but that doesn't mean scouts write off players who possess these traits. A high school player who is physical and has elite strength can still improve and get even stronger over time.

Body Indicators and Examining Height / Weight

A player's body, from the size of their feet and hands to their overall body shape and construction, can help scouts project a player's future potential in baseball.

One night in Smyrna, TN, Sonny Gray was pitching. He was one of the players in my area I really wanted, so I would go see him every chance I could. This particular night, there were about 60-70 scouts to see him. Somehow, I found myself behind home plate with none other than Jack Z. We were watching the game, talking, and catching up, but careful not to discuss players.

Suddenly, the lights went out in the ballpark, and it was going to be a while before they would come back on. Usually, in this situation, the pitcher is done for the night and doesn't come back out when the game resumes. So, most of the scouts left the ballpark, but a few stayed, including Jack and me.

We ended up talking to a young boy who wearing a Brewers hat. This kid proceeded to break it all down, including that his favorite player was Joe Dillon. Jack and I talked to this young man for about an hour about Joe, why he was his favorite, and everything he liked about the game.

And you know what? The lights went back on, and Sonny Gray went back out to pitch. To be completely accurate, he didn't just pitch. He dominated. I was sold. The separators here for Sonny were makeup and fearlessness. The will to win was at elite levels. And all he's done since then is exactly that.

Athleticism, athletic markers, tools, skills, makeup, and body are all important pieces to the puzzle. MLB players come in all shapes and sizes, from towering figures like Aaron Judge to more compact players like Jose Altuve. Players like Dustin Pedroia, Sonny Gray, and David Eckstein have also proven that size doesn't always dictate success.

Current Height / Weight Combo

Height and weight are among the first things to analyze when projecting a player's potential. Once scouts see a player's height and weight on a roster or scout book, they start to get an idea of what the player looks like and can make an educated guess about their potential before even seeing them play.

Every human body has a unique threshold for how height and weight work together to create an optimal athlete. The goal is for players to reach their optimal balance between height and weight around age 26. So, a player who looks gangly or disproportionate in high school may still have room to grow and mature into the athlete you see on TV.

Every height typically has an ideal weight, but present strength and physicality may not always reflect the ideal prospect. Scouts have to project a player's "Max" strength. Because one thing that can improve over time is their strength; they can get in the weight room. There's still time for natural physical maturity. They can still get bigger. A physically imposing player in high school can still get stronger without sacrificing athleticism. For example, Derek Jeter's frame in high school suggested he had plenty of room to gain weight and get stronger without losing athleticism.

Scouts also consider athletic markers and other factors. Generally speaking, a high school prospect listed at 6'3" / 155 pounds likely has room to get much stronger without sacrificing athleticism. But if a player appears to be maxed out physically, it's a little bit of a red flag.

Every player has projection left until they reach their full potential. A position player who is 6'2" / 225 in high school can still be athletic and have projection. However, if a hitter at this size wants to reach their full potential, they must display elite raw strength now. It's difficult to project a player to develop the required strength down the road when they are already 6'2"/250+.

Prince Fielder is an excellent example of an early bloomer who displayed elite raw power, strength, and athleticism in high school. He didn't require much projection to know that he had the potential to become a dominant player. As he grew and got stronger, his raw power continued to flourish, making him an even more formidable force on the field. Signed by Tom Mcnamara with Jack Zduriencik as the scouting director, Fielder's athleticism was identified as the separator rather than the other tools some may expect.

Limbs, Levers, Hands, and Feet

Scouts also look at a player's limbs, or "levers," to see if they can generate more leverage in their movements. For example, long levers can be especially useful for pitchers who want to throw the ball faster and farther.

Similarly, a player with long legs may be able to take longer strides and run faster.

Long levers that stand out from the body can indicate that the player is still growing or can hold more weight on their frame.

A player's feet and hands can also be important indicators. Large feet may suggest that the player's body hasn't finished growing yet, while large hands indicate a player who can comfortably grip different pitches. For example, Edwin Diaz's ability to wrap his entire hand around a baseball was a key indicator of his selection in the MLB draft. This particular assessment is what's known as a veteran move. Joe McIlvaine, a long-time GM who drafted Darryl Strawberry and Dwight Gooden, among others, tested Edwin with this in Puerto Rico. Knowing that Mariners Area Supervisor Noel Sevilla and Puerto Rico scout Rafael Santo Domingo believed in the future All-Star closer now known as "Sugar," Joe performed this test and made sure to fight for Edwin in the draft because he believed in Edwin's ability to throw hard one day.

Athleticism, Explosiveness, and Ease

Beyond a player's physical appearance, scouts analyze their athleticism, explosiveness, and ease of movement. These traits come in all shapes and sizes, and a player's appearance can be deceiving, so scouts focus on key indicators beneath the surface.

For example, players like Pete Alonso, Daniel Vogelbach, and Prince Fielder may not have had the "perfect" body, but they all had strength in their wrists, explosiveness, and the ability to hit the ball well, which are the indicators that scouts look for.

Ease of delivery is a major indicator of projection for pitchers. An easy delivery can indicate a player's potential upside, role on the team, and even longevity.

Overall Future Potential (OFP)

OFP is the final score assigned to a player, and this vital metric reveals a player's potential role and ceiling in their baseball career. OFP is like a secret code, a grading system that translates a player's abilities into something tangible and specific.

One night in Nashville, I was sitting with Twins scouting director Deron Johnson and Professional Scouting Coordinator Vern Followell (still the best name for a scout ever, as he follows well). We're breaking down players for our first pick. I'm in full question mode, searching for answers on pretty much everything.

We talk about a player who was projected to go at the top of the draft, maybe as high as first overall. I'm in, largely because I'm supposed to be, on the bat. While breaking down the player, I asked Vern if he would take this player where we selected. He said, "I would, but I wouldn't be happy about it."

Vern spent the next 15-20 minutes analyzing the things in this player's game that gave him pause. DJ pulled out his phone and showed me video of a player in high consideration for our pick. The differences in athleticism, ceiling, and age were striking. The next day at the ballpark, we watched this player (and others) again. This time, armed with new knowledge, I saw what Vern was talking about. That player went far before we picked, and the player in the video was available at our selection. We took the guy we wanted, and his career has been undeniably better than the player Vern wasn't "happy" with. Ceiling and future role were the defining factors.

As a building block in shaping a draft board, OFP directly connects to a role and the round in which a player is typically chosen. Before we delve deeper into the world of OFP, let's explore more about this fascinating metric:

OFP employs the same 20-80 range as the standard scouting scale, providing a familiar framework for scouts and teams.

To calculate OFP, add individual grades and divide by the total number of grades considered.

Because OFP focuses on a player's future potential, there's no need for a "present/future" OFP; it's a single score derived from future grades.

OFP/Role Grading Scale	
20	No Value
30	Marginal / Up and Down through the system
40	Backup player / Starter on a losing team
45	Backup on *Championship team/Regular on 2nd place team
50	Starter on *Championship team
55	Above average regular starter, OCC all-star
60	All-Star
70	Perennial All-Star
80	Hall of Famer

A championship team is defined as a team that will win a pennant. This is a team that will compete for championships.

A player's OFP can provide insight into a young athlete's future trajectory, helping determine their potential impact on a championship team and guiding decision-making during drafting.

Before calculating a player's OFP, scouts will determine which position a player will most likely play at the Big League level. Then, they can use the positional profile table to weigh each tool, providing a clearer picture of their overall potential.

In rare instances, I come across players who project as super-utility types, like Ben Zobrist. Unique athletes with the versatility to play multiple positions are invaluable assets to a team. A super-utility player must have the skills to play shortstop, a powerful indicator of their adaptability on the diamond, and should exhibit exceptional instincts, setting them apart from their peers.

When evaluating a super-utility player, I try to project their best positional fit on the field, focusing on where they'll play most often and calculating their OFP based on that position. While not used much today, If you find yourself talking players with a veteran scout and he asks your opinion, drop a number like 52 In your eval and he will know what you mean.

Defining a Player's Ceiling and Floor

In baseball scouting, "ceiling" refers to the maximum potential or the highest level of performance a player could achieve in their career. It represents an estimation of the best possible outcome for a player, considering their current skill set, athleticism, and projected development.

Evaluating a player's ceiling helps scouts and teams make informed decisions when selecting players for their roster, weighing the potential rewards against the risks associated with drafting and developing prospects.

A high ceiling is ideal because it indicates that a player has the potential to become something truly special. Many players possess a high ceiling, but success is not guaranteed; it depends on work ethic, adaptability, coaching, and even luck.

A high floor indicates a player's likelihood to become a solid, reliable contributor to a team, even if they may not develop into a superstar or achieve exceptional performance levels. *Floor* represents a more conservative estimation of a player's abilities, considering their current skill set and baseline consistency.

A player can have a high floor and a low ceiling, making them a safer pick with limited potential for exceptional performance. Conversely, a player with a high ceiling and a low floor is considered a riskier choice – the "hit or miss" type.

Role Projection

Determining a player's potential impact at the Major League level requires a scout to project a player's role accurately.

For example, scouts consider whether a pitcher will become an ace or a backend rotation pitcher, reliever, closer, or an innings eater.

When evaluating position players, the primary focus is their potential impact, especially up the middle, positions like catcher, shortstop, and centerfielder. Batting and defensive capabilities should be considered when establishing their overall role profile.

Some players with strong batting skills may be unable to play shortstop, and these players might need to switch to second, third, left field, or another position. Conversely, some players with excellent defensive abilities struggle with hitting and will hold more value in central positions or as versatile utility players.

These two extremes – "bat only" and the "glove only" players – deviate from the central focus of determining a player's position and offensive impact. Scouts must assess whether their skills will be sufficient for their position in the context of the entire team.

Evaluating a player's athleticism, foot range, and versatility helps determine if they can have a post in a premium position or need to switch. A player's position may impose greater requirements for specific tools or skills.

Will they be a leadoff hitter or a power hitter driving in runs? Accurate role projection enables an organization to understand who they're drafting and how they will fit into the team dynamics.

Fallback Roles

A fallback role or "Plan B" outlining how a player can contribute to the organization is necessary if the player doesn't reach their ceiling or struggles. These players typically possess excellent instincts, aptitude, makeup, and a natural feel for the game, enabling them to transition successfully.

I document a player's mental toughness and ability to adapt to a new position. Some organizations may not require this information in a scouting report, but I believe they should be aware of a player's flexibility and potential for contributing if things don't go as planned.

Two-way players are examples of individuals with fallback roles. Athletes capable of pitching and playing a position are drafted every year. Most organizations prefer players to devote their time to a single skill set. However, if the player struggles in their original position, knowing they can also contribute on the mound is beneficial.

By recognizing and documenting potential fallback roles, I provide a more comprehensive understanding of a player's potential for my organization to use during the drafting and development process.

Injury history

Another element to scouting prospects is to be well-informed about a player's injury history. Freak accidents and random events can occur but generally don't affect a player's long-term value. Broken bones and strains with clear recovery paths are usually not a significant concern.

However, recurring injuries affecting the same body part can raise red flags. Repeated sprained ankles, recurring hamstring issues, or persistent tendinitis in a pitcher would be worrisome. Major injuries, such as torn ACLs or those requiring Tommy

John surgery, are also causes for concern and necessitate regular updates on the player's status and recovery progress.

The old saying, "You can't make the club in the tub," rings true in the world of scouting.

Player Comparisons

Comparing a prospect or a young player to a current or former big-league player paints a picture of the prospect's potential future role, skill set, and impact at the Major League level.

Using player comps gives coaches, front office personnel, and other decision-makers a quick, relatable reference that offers insight into the player's potential.

A scout must have an extensive mental database of big-league players to draw upon for quick and concise references and player comparisons.

When creating a player comp, I note the appropriate handedness (lefty/righty), body type, attributes, and profile. The player comp should align with the OFP to ensure consistency. For example, if I say a player reminds me of Rickey Henderson, he shouldn't have a 50 OFP, as that would be a mismatch.

Not all MLB organizations require player comps on scouting reports, so scouts usually follow their organization's preferences.

Chapter 8

The Intangibles: Work Ethic, Mental Toughness, and More

Many factors influence why some players can carry their tools into the games, so intangibles are also included in an evaluation. Traditional means of quantifying traits like make-up, maturity, intestinal fortitude, adjustability, and work ethic are not available, but the scout sees them. These factors can influence a player's ability to handle adversity, adapt to the professional game, and reach their full potential.

It's a big mistake to think that a scout only watches you on the field. Scouts also pay close attention to a player's actions during practices, warm-ups, and interactions with teammates and coaches. Always put forth your best effort and exhibit a strong work ethic, regardless of the setting. Demonstrating consistency and professionalism on and off the field will leave a lasting impression on scouts.

I look for players who can handle pressure, stay focused in adversity, and inspire their teammates to achieve greatness. These x-factors have proven to reduce my margin of error and make me more efficient in predicting whether a player can reach their potential.

Makeup

Makeup is the intangible quality that can make or break a player's potential, and I feel it is the most important factor in determining if a talented, drafted player will reach his ceiling.

Scouts look for a combination of character, intensity, focus, competitiveness, and how a player interacts with others on and off the field.

A player's character shapes their behavior on the field and in the clubhouse. They should know right from wrong and have a strong work ethic. Players with good character are more likely to behave appropriately; players with bad character will struggle when faced with challenges.

Intensity, focus, and competitiveness translate into a player's work ethic, early and late work, studying, video analysis, and building game libraries. A player with a strong desire to compete and excel is more likely to work toward improving their skills and succeeding on the field.

Beyond a player's physical abilities, I evaluate their overall makeup for success at the next level.

Love of the Game and Your Position

A player who genuinely enjoys playing the game and has a passion for competition and a desire to be the best can set themselves apart from others.

It's really difficult to be great at something you don't enjoy. I want a player who loves the game of baseball – they can't get enough of it, they want to be around it, they want to work at it, and it's fun to them. I avoid guys who don't seem to love being around the game or feel that practice is a chore or an obligation, not another opportunity to be around the game.

Loving the game usually leads to a good work ethic. With 162 games per season, you have to love it.

I want players who love to hit or pitch and don't play a position just because they happen to be good at it. A player who loves hitting but was forced to be a pitcher doesn't have the same love for it and doesn't enjoy the practices or have the same intensity on the mound.

Facing Adversity

I look for players who have faced adversity, love competition, and have a knack for bouncing back. Baseball is a failure-driven game – especially hitting. And if a player has never faced adversity or good competition, there is some unknown as to how they will react when it comes. Every player in baseball will get shelled on the mound or slump at the plate, and the ones who have had nothing but success and an easy route sometimes don't bounce back well when it happens.

Baseball is a game of failure; even the best players fail more often than they succeed. That's why scouts look for players who have faced adversity, have a positive attitude, a growth mindset, and are willing to work to improve.

But it's not just about being positive; it's also about having a burning desire to succeed. Players who truly love the game and are willing to do whatever it takes to improve will be the ones who will reach their potential. They have a hunger that can't be satisfied, and they use failure to fuel them forward.

Aptitude/Adjustability

As players climb up the ranks of baseball, their raw athleticism and talent won't be enough to dominate their competition. They must learn to apply new information, adapt to new circumstances, and excel. Another way of thinking about aptitude is adjustability.

Many players, throughout their young lives, were by far the best player on their team or in their league. Their athleticism and raw tools are dominant over their peers. But the farther they go in the game, the tougher competition will challenge them in ways they've never experienced.

There will be a moment when they are in awe of their competition. A hitter will reference that this pitcher "blew his doors off" with elite velocity. Or a pitcher will get "shelled" after dominating his entire life because, up until then, he was "the elite."

This is where aptitude comes in. Players who can't adjust to higher pitch velocity or struggle with new coaching will struggle to make it in professional baseball. The key to success is making adjustments, getting feedback, receiving coaching well, and applying it. Without aptitude, players will continue to struggle and eventually get released.

Scouts look for players who have the tools and physical attributes, good character, and are coachable. They are willing to listen and learn from others, whether their coaches or teammates. They are humble and willing to put the team first rather than their personal goals.

As a parent of a promising young baseball player, remember that it's not just about talent. Players must have the right mindset, work ethic, and character. If your child has those qualities, they have a chance to succeed at the highest level.

I know you want to help your child succeed in baseball, so encourage them to develop their aptitude and adjustability skills. This will be the difference between those who succeed and those who don't. Remember, the greats are not just physically gifted but mentally adaptable.

Chapter 9

The Scouting Report - Putting It All Together

As you've read, a scout's job is to discover talented ballplayers AND accurately assess their abilities. Scouts evaluate players based on their physical tools, baseball skills, and intangible qualities that contribute to their overall potential and performance on the field.

Scouts have to keep meticulous notes on every player we are tracking as a prospect so that we have the data to back up what goes into the scouting reports.

I'll never forget the first time Hall of Fame scout Larry Corrigan walked up to me at a game and said, "Jeremy, show me your cards," referring to the game cards we would make our notes on. We were both with the Twins at the time, so I would show him my cards. As if he was possessed by an evil grammar school teacher, he immediately started picking my notes apart, "This is wrong, and that's wrong – you gotta get this right – and circle this one – highlight this…. Where is your multi-colored pen, Jeremy? Do you have your multi-colored pen?" I said, "No, Larry, I don't have a multi-colored pen." With a sigh of exasperation, he shot back, "You have to have your multi-colored pen. How are you going to highlight anything?"

Is he for real? Was this guy messing with me? "Larry, what are you talking about?" I asked.

He said, "Look, the first time around that you see a guy, it's in black ink; next time, it's red, and then green, and then blue... Just get one of these multi-colored pens!"

It turns out that Larry was exceptionally good at this. It taught me that your card wasn't just your notes. It was your life. Because when you go back to write your reports, you've got all your information right there, color-coded.

It's kind of a running joke in the scouting industry with Larry. Apparently, I'm not the only one to get this lesson. I bet any scout reading this will laugh because they've either been through it or heard about Larry "Show Me Your Cards" Corrigan.

Some might say his motives were less about sharing his knowledge than about getting a peek at what others were seeing in players.

Fast forward a few years later, I was with the Brewers scouting at Baylor University, and I ran into Larry, who was with the Pirates at that time. Without missing a beat, he says, "Hey Jeremy, show me your cards." I said, "Absolutely not, Larry." "Why not?" he asked, seemingly offended. I said, "Uh, we're not working for the same team anymore. You're not seeing my notes." He just grinned and said, "That-a-boy, good job."

When creating an MLB scouting report, I focus on the most relevant information so the decision-makers can select players who have the potential to become future stars. My reports also provide valuable feedback to players and coaches on areas where they can improve their game.

Here's a breakdown of a typical baseball scouting report:

Tim Anderson (SS)
Amateur Scouting - Position Report

Final OFP:	58.00	Category: Strong Average	Class: J2	ML Pos: SS	ML Role: Reg		Probable:
Scout: Jeremy Booth		Date Observed: 3/26/2013	Games Seen: 3	Def Innings: 21	At Bats: 15		Workouts: HS FR

Player Details

DOB: 6/23/1993	School: East Central CC	Current Pos: SS			B / T: Right / Right
HT / WT: 6'1" / 180	State: MS	Eyewear:			Hand Size: Medium
Last Seen: 3/26/2013	Grad Date: 6/1/2013	Area Scout: Dustin Evans			Cross Checker:

Physical Description:	lean, wiry, sloped shoulders, long arms, high waist, average hands and feet	
Athleticism:	Excellent	Comments: fast twitch, explosive
Player Comparison	Shawon Dunston	

Medical Issues:	

Makeup

quiet, competes, hustles, leads by example

Ratings

	Present	Future	Comments
Hitting Ability:	45	60	stays inside the ball, bat speed, plate coverage, leverage, consistent contact
Plate Discipline:	50	55	has an approach, sees the ball, stays within his zone
Raw Power:	50	55	pull side power, creates pop with leverage and bat speed
Power Production:	40	50	will drive mistakes to the pull side
Arm Strength:	50	55	online carry, loose arm, more as he matures and adds strength
Arm Accuracy:	50	50	has touch and feel
Fielding Ability:	45	55	has instincts, body control, ok footwork, reads
Body Control:	70	70	handles himself well, keeps everything together
Range:	50	60	good to both sides, changes direction on a dime
Running Speed:	70	70	fast twitch, good stride, explosive, light feet, extra gear
Home to 1B:	70	70	gets out of the box, turns it on when he smells a hit
Base Running:	50	60	ok jumps, looks to run, has instincts and reads

Assets

Risk Factor:	0	still raw, has ceiling
KHTP:	0	has instincts, feel for the game
Determination:	1	dials it up a notch when the situation has importance

OFP Calculation Result

Base OFP:	57.67	+ Assets:	0.33	+ Separator:	0	= Final OFP:	58.00	OFP Category:	Strong Average
Separator Comments:									

Running Times

Left: 0.00	Right: 4.10	40 Yrd: 0	60 Yrd: 0.00	Cat Rel: 0

Summary

REG SS in ML role. Has Middle of the diamond value in speed, instincts, and athleticism. Lean loose body with plenty of life. Still raw but has ceiling and instincts that show game feel. Good body control and explosiveness. Has plus bat speed when he wants it, and appears to be slowing his game down against inferior competition. Dials it up when he has a chance at driving in runs or faces a pitcher with velocity. Has a loose swing with extra base potential. Pull side power in his future. Good baserunner that looks to run with ok jumps when stealing. Has quick and light feet that make up for some technical flaws. Has instincts with reads on hops and field awareness. Works on his game in practice and doesn't waste reps. Have to be patient but he will reward you. Just 19 as a JC sophomore.

Round:	1	Would Take: 1	Must Take: 1A	Signability:		Agent:
Entry Level: RA		ETA: 2018	Dual Sport:	Signability Comments:		

Physical Tools	Assessment of a player's physical attributes, such as height, weight, and overall athleticism. These attributes can impact a player's performance, durability, and potential for growth. Key factors include speed, arm strength, and power.
Baseball Skills	Detailed evaluation of a player's baseball-specific skills is imperative. For position players, this includes hitting, fielding, and base running abilities. For pitchers, scouts focus on pitch variety, velocity, control, and overall command of the strike zone. Scouts will often use a grading scale (usually 20-80) to rate these skills, with higher numbers indicating greater proficiency.
Intangible Qualities	Intangible qualities, including work ethic, attitude, leadership, baseball IQ, and mental toughness, can significantly impact a player's success on and off the field. These can be difficult to quantify but are necessary to determine a player's potential to adapt, improve, and contribute to a team's success.
Performance History	Statistics, awards, and notable achievements from a player's past performance, providing context and demonstrating their performance against various levels of competition.

Injury History	Note any past injuries and the player's recovery process which can impact a player's future performance and durability.
Projected Development	Projections on how a player is expected to develop over time, including areas for improvement and potential ceilings, which assists teams in making player development and investment decisions.
Comparison to Current or Former Players	Scouts frequently draw comparisons between a prospect and current or former major league players to provide context for a player's potential performance and help teams envision how a prospect might fit into their organization.

I create concise summaries of all the information I've gathered over time. For example, I might mention that a player has the potential to hit in the middle of the lineup and become an all-star shortstop. However, it's generally not necessary to include specific details like the heights and weights of the player's parents or the precise grip they use for certain pitches.

I will assign two grades to each tool: a current grade and a future grade. This is usually denoted with a slash '/'. For example, I might say a player's arm is a 40/60, where "40" represents the current grade and "60" indicates the future grade for what the arm is projected to be.

Remember, "Projection" refers to what the arm will become during the player's prime years.

Understanding the criteria scouts use to evaluate players can help you focus on the areas that matter most in your development. To position themselves to catch the attention of scouts and succeed in their baseball journey, players should hone the five tools, develop their baseball IQ, and showcase strong intangibles.

Along with raw talent, scouts want to see players who demonstrate a deep understanding of the game and a commitment to continuous improvement. Prioritize developing your tools, baseball IQ, and mental makeup to become the type of player that scouts and coaches seek.

The scouting process is ongoing, and scouts always look for players who demonstrate growth and progress. Use this knowledge to your advantage, and continually work on refining your skills and mindset—on and off the field.

Finally, remember that while the scouting process can be complex and sometimes intimidating, it's also an opportunity to showcase your abilities and make your dreams a reality. Embrace the challenge, stay focused on your goals, and trust your abilities. With hard work, dedication, and a little luck, you might find yourself on the radar of professional baseball scouts and one step closer to the big leagues.

Every player is unique, and each athlete's path to success may look different. Scouts are searching for potential as much as they are looking for current performance. Showcasing your dedication to improvement, adaptability, and passion for the game will set you apart from the competition.

Chapter 10

Maximizing Exposure –
How Pro Scouts Find
and Track Players to Watch

The two most common questions I get from parents are:

1. What are you looking for in a player?
2. How do you find players?

Well, everything you've read so far should answer question 1. But to sum it up…

I'm looking for the "fire within." I want players who demonstrate an unwavering passion for the game, an inner drive that pushes them to excel and improve every single day. This burning desire is evident in the way a player practices, communicates with teammates, and interacts with coaches. Showcase that unrelenting passion to capture my attention.

Pitchers – I'm looking for guys that throw strikes. That compete in the strike zone. That can mix pitches. That have good stuff. That hang zeroes on the scoreboard and get outs.

Hitters – I'm looking for guys with BARREL TO BALL SKILLS. Guys that don't swing and miss a ton. Guys that can really get the barrel on the ball and hit balls hard in games vs. fastballs, breaking balls, and changeups.

To answer question 2.

If you can do one of these two things against elite competition, I want to find you. Let's make it easy for both of us.

Navigating the world of scouting isn't easy, and figuring out which opportunities are the real deal can be overwhelming. In this chapter, I will clear up some myths and misconceptions and talk about the most common ways players find their way onto a scout's tracking list.

Getting Scouted for The Draft
– Separating Fact from Fiction

Myth #1: Playing on a high school team is the best way to get scouted.

Scouting can be quite a meticulous and time-consuming task, so I'm always striving for ways to make it more efficient. My main goal is to witness as many players in action as frequently as possible. It would be ideal to attend events where I can see multiple prospects, preferably competing against one another.

Now, when it comes to finding new players, high school games aren't exactly the most efficient option for professional scouts. These games usually have a limited number of prospects within a specific geographic area, which makes it challenging to identify and evaluate a wide range of talent. Plus, the level of competition in high school games can vary greatly, making it difficult to gauge a player's true potential based solely on their performance in these settings.

However, high school games do offer a valuable opportunity for scouts to watch prospects they're already keeping tabs on. It allows us to gather more information and form a comprehensive assessment of a player's skills and potential. High school games may not be the best for discovering new talent, but they still play an important role in the scouting process.

I would typically attend high school games to evaluate a known prospect's in-game performance and see how they handle pressure, their approach to different situations, and their ability to adjust. There are instances where another player who wasn't on my radar before shows me something that puts them on my list. So just because a scout isn't there to see you doesn't mean you are invisible.

High school coaches can be incredibly valuable sources of information for understanding a player's skills, work ethic, character, and potential for growth. They have the advantage of spending a significant amount of time with their players, both during practices and in other aspects of their lives. They can provide insights into a player's demeanor, level of commitment, and overall attitude toward the game.

Scouts need to strike a balance between trusting the opinions of coaches and independently verifying the information through their own evaluation. While coaches offer valuable perspectives, scouts have to rely on their own judgment. As the saying goes, "Trust but verify."

There is a big misconception that if you haven't been scouted by your junior year in high school, you missed the boat. Don't fall into the trap of thinking it's too late to be scouted if you haven't been noticed by your junior year of high school. Early exposure can be beneficial, but scouts know players develop at different rates. Late bloomers often emerge with newfound skills and potential in their senior year or beyond, catching the eyes of scouts. I encourage you to stay persistent, keep improving, and never give up on your dreams.

Scouts want to find talent wherever it exists. Still, most won't attend high school games unless it's to see a prospect they have been tracking or there are at least one or more players that someone in their network they trust has been talking up.

If getting recruited to play in college is your goal, remember that your high school season is going on while college coaches and recruiters are focusing on their season, which significantly limits their scouting time.

Summer showcases, tournaments, and travel team events provide a more optimal environment for college coaches to discover new talent because they bring together a large number of talented players from various regions in a single location.

If you're a standout player in high school, your skills will not go unnoticed, but carefully selecting a travel team and attending individual combines can amplify your exposure.

Even if you play for a small school in a small town, if you're that good, scouts come to you, but only if they know about you.

Myth 2: Scouts Find Players by Looking at Stats

I know how easily a player can become fixated on statistics. However, don't be fooled by the myth that scouts scour through game numbers to find their next prospect. While I can get some valuable insights from stats, they don't come close to painting the complete picture of a player's potential. I have to look well beyond the numbers, evaluating physical tools, intangible qualities such as work ethic, mental toughness, baseball IQ, and overall growth trajectory.

Stats are useful for tracking progress; remember that scouts see the bigger picture, and so should you. Focus on your overall skills, mechanics, and potential for growth. Concentrate on improving your game and showcasing your abilities.

Scouts understand that an amateur player's stats must be taken with a grain of salt. The level of competition, quality of coaching, and even weather conditions can all impact a player's stats, so scouts look beyond those numbers to evaluate the whole picture.

Let's face it… the level of competition a player is up against is a major variable in what stats can tell me. Raw data like exit velocity is indisputable, but other stats like ERA and batting average must be considered in context. Strikeouts and walks are good indicators of a hitter's contact. A good scout can see beyond a lower-than-expected batting average, knowing the best of the best have all had a string of bad luck.

Consistent performance doesn't necessarily mean hitting a specific number of home runs or maintaining a certain batting average. Instead, scouts look for hitters who consistently perform well by limiting strikeouts and drawing walks and for pitchers who can induce soft contact and generate swings and misses.

I want to see a player's progress over time. Showcasing consistent improvement and a strong work ethic can make a lasting impression, even if the stats aren't eye-popping.

I prioritize a player's overall skills and physical tools over raw statistics. I'm more interested in a pitcher's fastball velocity, command, and secondary pitches than in their ERA. Focus on developing your skills, and the stats will follow.

As players progress through baseball, some make minor improvements while others undergo significant development. Scouts aim to envision a player's potential growth, while player development ensures that vision becomes a reality.

Myth 3: Only the Top-Ranked Players Get Drafted

Rankings can help gauge a player's potential, but they're not the be-all and end-all for the MLB draft. They can play a role in catching a scout's attention, but rankings are not the deciding factor in whether to come to see you. Some front office personnel may follow lists or rankings, but most professional clubs make their evaluations and decisions based on a player's skill set, performance, and potential.

Some clubs may view lists as a way to identify players they may not have seen before, but good organizations won't let these rankings dictate their draft strategy or decision-making process.

They recognize that scouting is much more than just following someone else's list.

Being ranked might help you get noticed initially, but you should focus on developing your skills and demonstrating your abilities on the field. Your performance and potential will attract the attention of scouts to get drafted potentially.

I rely on my evaluations and often unearth hidden gems that fly under the radar. Stay focused on your growth, and don't worry too much about your ranking. If you're that good, I'll find you.

Summer of Opportunity – The Direct Path to Exposure

The formula for getting exposure is pretty simple. You need to go to where the scouts and college coaches are instead of waiting for them to come to you.

The summer between junior and senior years of high school is the prime window for getting discovered by pro scouts and college coaches. Use this time to make the most noise and get in front of as many scouts as possible to increase your chances of being drafted by the pros or recruited for college.

To maximize my exposure to top talent, I prioritize attending premier showcases, tournaments, camps, and combines through-out the summer. Scouts attend these events to watch prospects playing against high-level competition, giving players some of the best opportunities to spotlight their abilities and potential for success in collegiate or professional baseball.

Travel Teams

I'm more interested in an individual player's abilities and potential than in which team they play for or its win/loss record. The real value part of a quality travel team is that they attract the attention of scouts because we know their rosters are filled with talented players who compete against strong competition.

Following these travel teams allows me to monitor the progress of elite prospects and observe their performance against other high-caliber players. This helps me determine if a player has the potential to succeed at higher levels of baseball and whether I should put them on my list for further scouting during the upcoming high school season.

Playing for a quality team doesn't necessarily mean playing for a "Big Name" team. I've watched too many players and families pay a ton of money to have their hopes and expectations mismanaged because they make the mistake of choosing a travel team that focuses on playing in 'Trophy Mill' tournaments against watered-down competition so they can pad their reputation with a meaningless win/loss record.

Choosing a well-regarded organization that has your best interests at heart and helps promote you is more important than playing for a "big-name" team. Scouts care about your performance and tools, not the team you play for.

Identifying the right travel team for maximum exposure and development

Research the coaching staff. The coaching staff plays a vital role in your child's development as a baseball player. Look for teams with experienced and knowledgeable coaches who are well-respected in the baseball community. The ideal coach should have a successful track record and be committed to helping players grow both on and off the field.

Balance of player development with exposure. Select a travel team that emphasizes player development and exposure. A team that provides access to professional skill development and opportunities to be seen by scouts and college coaches will help your child reach their full potential. Choose travel teams that participate in competitive tournaments, attend player development combines, and bring in professional scouts to evaluate their players.

Assess team reputation. Talk to other parents, coaches, and players who have experience with the team. Pay attention to a team's off-field culture and their alumni's success getting drafted by the pros or recruited to play in college. A positive, supportive environment that fosters teamwork and personal growth is invaluable for a young athlete.

Logistics. Travel, accommodations, and scheduling can significantly impact your family's summer plans. Look for a team that is upfront about the associated costs and has a manageable travel schedule. Make sure the team fits your family's needs and budget.

Participation in competitive events. The level of competition matters. To truly showcase their talent, players must compete against other top-notch players. When evaluating travel teams, examine their schedules to ensure they participate in high-profile tournaments and face off against elite teams. This will help your player improve and increase their chances of catching the eye of scouts who regularly attend these events.

Travel Team Showcases and Tournaments

Travel team events consisting of talented players from various regions allow scouts to evaluate a larger pool of athletes in one location and compare them head-to-head. They are particularly beneficial because scouts see how players perform against high-level competition, which is needed to dive deep into their potential at the next level.

As I said earlier, scouting is meticulous and time-consuming. One of the most ideal and efficient situations is when I can catch a game where a prospect pitcher faces a prospect hitter – in scouting, we call these games "matchups."

Matchups are beneficial for two reasons: scouts can observe multiple prospects during the same game and evaluate how they perform against equal talent levels. It's one thing to watch a top high school pitcher or hitter dominate their competition, but catching a glimpse of how a pitcher's stuff fares against skilled hitters can be incredibly insightful. When planning my scouting schedule, I prioritize finding these matchups.

Oh, and don't think that scouts are only watching during games. I get to games early to gather raw tool grades I might not have seen yet and watch pregame infield/outfield warmups for arm grades and batting practice for raw power grades. When tracking a player, I watch their entire routine and pre-game process. This tells me a lot about why a player is succeeding, failing, or even experiencing fatigue during games.

Individual Player Showcases, Camps, and Combines

Individual player events provide the distinct advantage of choosing which events best fit you as an individual player.

The right events will provide opportunities to receive individualized attention, often from former big leaguers, in a controlled environment, where drills, workouts, and simulated games are tailored to highlight players' abilities, making it easier for scouts to focus on each player.

Pro scouts and college coaches regularly attend camps and combines, which means more exposure for you. These events also create networking opportunities, allowing players to interact directly with college coaches and scouts and foster relationships that may lead to future opportunities.

You'll undoubtedly be bombarded with promotions to attend these kinds of events. Because there is a limited window, be selective and make educated decisions about which opportunities for exposure are best for you.

Identifying the Best Opportunities for Exposure to Scouts

One of the biggest myths is that you must attend every showcase event to get noticed.

Showcases can be valuable opportunities to get noticed by scouts; they can also be expensive and even detrimental. Overloading your schedule with showcases leads to burnout and diminished performance and can also cause *overexposure.*

Now that may seem counterintuitive but let me explain. When a player participates in too many events or showcases, scouts and evaluators may scrutinize them more closely and possibly magnify flaws in their game. Ultimately, overexposure becomes a concern when players participate in environments where their skills are picked apart due to the lack of competition on the field. Remember, quality trumps quantity when attending the right events during this summer of opportunity.

I've got to tell it like it is. Some popular events are considered "Must Attend," but they don't make much sense to me—for example, showcase tournaments with 400 teams playing games spread across an entire state. Realistically, you probably won't get seen by many, if any, scouts until the playoffs. So, if you are a pitcher, for example, and your team burns you in the first couple of days, even if you were lights out and helped them get to the playoffs, it doesn't matter because no scouts were there to see it.

Consider these two factors to determine if an event is worth attending:

1. **Quality over quantity:** Attending a few well-regarded events rather than many lower-tier events is better. Focus on events known for attracting scouts and college coaches where you can showcase your skills and abilities while facing intense competition for a better chance to be seen by scouts and college coaches.

   High-level combines also provide social media coverage through live streams or video, giving players widespread exposure to scouts who can't attend the event onsite.

2. **Competition level:** Choose events with a high level of competition. Scouts are more likely to attend events where they can see several prospects simultaneously. Participating in tournaments or showcases featuring top talent will increase your chances of being noticed.

No single path guarantees success, and the key is to be proactive and take advantage of every real opportunity that comes your way. Stay committed to your development as a player, continually work on your skills, and maintain a strong work ethic on and off the field.

When I am interested in a player, and especially when making a decision about a player, I know that I'm never truly done evaluating them. Continuously watching their performance, habits, and growth helps me to make the most accurate assessments possible.

There's no such thing as a single make-or-break event.

Players identified from open combines and camps may be invited to signature events that increase their opportunities to gain exposure. But don't sweat it if you have a bad outing or don't make the cut for every elite showcase.

Some players didn't shine during the summer but still made it big. Take Justin Lange, for example. He didn't perform exceptionally well in the summer, but after a strong high school senior season, he was selected 34th overall by the Padres in the 2020 Draft. Then there's Grayson Rodriguez, who, like Lange, didn't make the Texas Area Code team (both played in the event with teams representing other regions) but still took part in different events and made considerable strides in his development. Now, he's playing in the big leagues with the Baltimore Orioles. Both these guys had so-so summers, but when they played at the New Balance Future Stars Series Main Events that fall, the work they put in to grow came through. It's all about looking beyond the obvious when scouting, and for me, putting these guys on the big stage led to great things. Those are solid examples of finding the right events for you at the right time and owning your process.

There's no shortage of stories like these, so don't ever think that the scouting process is over just because you didn't make it into a specific event or round. Put yourself on the map in some way to ensure that you've been identified. From there, it's up to you.

You will be noticed if your skills align with what scouts are looking for. Get started and make the most of the right opportunities that come your way.

The most important thing to remember is that every player is different. Your path to success will be unique, so don't worry about what everyone else is doing. Keep working hard, stay dedicated to the game, and always be open to learning and growing.

Word of Mouth

Never underestimate the power of others talking about you. When players start making a name for themselves on the field and within the baseball community, people talk. A strong reputation can go a long way in catching the attention of scouts.

Building Relationships and Networking within the Industry

Good scouts lean on a solid network of relationships with high school and college coaches, travel team organizers, and other baseball insiders. Their recommendations can be a valuable source of information for scouts to identify potential prospects.

The scouting community is very tight. They constantly exchange information, share insights, and keep an ear to the ground for the latest buzz on up-and-coming talent.

Parents should encourage their players to cultivate relationships within the baseball community. The more people you know, the more opportunities you'll have to showcase your skills and get noticed by the right people.

Social Media

With the increasing availability of video footage and online resources, scouts can research and evaluate players remotely. While nothing beats seeing a player in person, finding a good clear video in a batting cage, bullpen session, or a combine workout on Twitter has earned more than a few players a place on my watch list.

Here are a few tips on using social media platforms like Twitter, Facebook, Instagram, and LinkedIn to connect and engage with people in the baseball industry and get the attention of scouts.

Create professional profiles. Set up public accounts on popular platforms (e.g., Twitter, Instagram, Facebook) dedicated to showcasing your baseball skills, achievements, and journey. Use a clear profile picture and write a concise bio highlighting your position, high school, and graduation year.

Share content regularly. Post videos of your training sessions, games, and highlights, showcasing your skills and progress. Include stats, awards, or any other relevant accomplishments in the comments. Don't forget to tag your team, coaches, and events you've attended.

Engage with the baseball community. Follow and interact with scouts, college coaches, teams, and fellow players. Engage in conversations, share your opinions on games or news, and congratulate others on their successes.

Use relevant hashtags and mentions. Use popular baseball-related hashtags to make your posts more discoverable and mention organizations, teams, or events related to your content.

Keep it positive. Your online reputation matters. Scouts and coaches look for players with good character, so show your sportsmanship, teamwork, and passion.

Network with peers and professionals. Connect with other players, coaches, and industry professionals. Engage with their content, make friends, and open doors to new opportunities.

Be proactive. Don't be shy! Reach out to scouts and coaches. Share your profile or highlight videos. Ask for advice or feedback and express your interest in their program or organization.

Networking is a long-term process, and it requires effort and persistence. But when you consistently put yourself out there, maintain connections, and demonstrate a genuine passion for the game, you'll attract attention, and the right people will keep you in mind.

Chapter 11

Recognizing When a Scout is Interested

Every young baseball player dreams of making it to the big leagues, but only a select few possess the exceptional talent, skill, and unwavering determination that catches the eye of professional scouts.

When a high school player manages to attract serious interest from a pro scout, it's truly a remarkable moment that could potentially change their lives and open the doors to a future in the major leagues. Let's look at some signs that might indicate a pro scout's interest in a player.

Frequent Attendance: If a scout shows up at multiple games, showcases, or practices where you're participating, it's a good indication that they're interested in you and are likely keeping a close eye on your performance, work ethic, and how you handle pressure situations.

Direct Communication: A scout may reach out to you, your coaches, or your parents to gather more information about your background, work ethic, and character. This direct communication is a strong indicator that they see potential in you and want to know more about your dedication and commitment to the sport.

Personal Interaction: If a scout approaches you after a game or during a showcase, it's a strong sign that they're considering you as a potential prospect. They may ask you questions about your playing experience, goals, or even your personal life. These interactions are an opportunity for the scout to assess your character and determine if you'd be a good fit for their organization.

Invitations to Exclusive Events: If you receive an invitation to attend a private workout, scout team event, or another exclusive baseball opportunity, it's a clear sign that a scout is interested in you. These events are typically reserved for players that scouts believe have the potential to succeed at the professional level.

In-Home Visits: Scouts with a serious interest in a player may schedule an in-home visit to meet the player and their family. During the visit, the scout will evaluate the player's character, work ethic, and family support system, because these factors can determine future success at the professional level.

If a scout shows signs of serious interest, maximize that interest and make it easy for them to see you as a real prospect. Here are a few tips to point you in the right direction:

Stay Consistent: Maintain a high level of performance and work ethic during games and practices. Scouts are interested in players who consistently demonstrate their skills and commitment to the sport. Showcasing your ability to perform under pressure can help capture and maintain a scout's interest.

Be Coachable: Show a willingness to learn and improve by actively seeking feedback from coaches and applying their advice to your game. Scouts want to see coachable players who have a strong desire to grow as athletes and individuals.

Showcase Your Character: Demonstrate good sportsmanship, leadership qualities, and a positive attitude both on and off the field. Players who can be successful in a team environment and contribute positively to the organization's culture will attract the attention of scouts. Your character can often be more important than your on-field abilities when being considered a potential prospect. A guy can have the tools, but he's just a bad person. And if you're a bad person, the tools never come out.

Stay in touch: Once you've established connections, make an effort to stay in touch. Reach out periodically to provide updates on your progress, ask for advice, or simply check in and maintain the connection. A simple message or phone call can go a long way in keeping relationships strong.

Decoding the "In-Home Visit" and Its Significance

The in-home represents a milestone in the scouting process. If there is strong interest, you can expect more than just the area scout to schedule an in-home visit. The goal is to understand the person behind the athlete, and these visits allow scouts to learn more about the player as an individual.

Substance is essential when evaluating potential players. Scouts must look beyond the surface and thoroughly research to understand a player's background, character, and support network.

I never rely solely on rumors or hearsay about a player, good or bad. Instead, I do my homework and verify the information. Home visits and personal interactions are necessary to gain insight into the player's family life and personal relationships.

It's part of my responsibility as a scout also to evaluate a player's off-field character, personal relationships, and support system. By doing so, I can better assess the likelihood of a player becoming a valuable asset to a team, ensuring a solid return on investment and ultimately contributing to the team's success.

One of the main things I want to come away from a home visit with is an understanding of how a player feels about himself. I want to get the bigger picture of where he sees himself fitting in after the draft and his thought process for determining whether he will sign with an organization.

In baseball scouting, we call this "Signability," and it's all about how likely it is that a player will sign a pro contract with the Major League Baseball team that drafted him.

Factors that could affect whether a player is signable might be a strong desire to finish their education or pressure from their family to go to college. There could be personal stuff going on in their life, or maybe their heart is set on a particular team.

The biggie is how much a player thinks they're worth compared to what the team will offer. Because if a player, or the people advising him, think he's worth more than what's on the table, he might decide not to sign. Maybe he'll go play in college and take another swing at the draft later on.

I was on a home visit with a particular player, and we were breaking down his summer, discussing where he stands in his class and his thoughts on being drafted out of high school vs. going to college. He was doing a great job, I was impressed. But then, out of nowhere, he says, "I want a million dollars."

Ok. I guess we can switch topics. So, I ask him, "When it comes to the draft, where do you think you fit? The top 30?"

"No," he says.

"The top 60?" I ask.

"Nah."

"Top 90?"

"Eh... No."

"How about the top 100?"

He said, "Yeah, somewhere around there, top 100, 110, maybe."

If his assessment was correct, that would put him near the 4th round. At that time, a million dollars would have been a back of the 1st round number.

So, I said, "Well, Mr. Player. What you're telling me is that you want a million dollars, but you don't think you are worth a million dollars."

He looked at me, kind of puzzled.

I said, "I'm not saying we have to answer the question today. But I need to understand something... You're telling me that if we select you in the fourth round, you want a million dollars, which is first-round money, even though you are telling me yourself that you are not anywhere close to being a first-round pick. Do I have this right?"

The puzzled look never left his face.

We ended the meeting. No hard feelings. He told me everything I needed to know about his signability.

Remember, an in-home visit signifies that scouts have recognized your potential and are eager to learn more about you. Your performance in your senior year of high school determines the extent of interest, so if you're a prospect they genuinely want to know, they'll make an effort to meet with you.

Treat an in-home visit as an opportunity to demonstrate maturity, character, and passion for baseball. Be open, honest, and respectful during the conversation. Let the scout know about the factors that will affect your decision.

Scouts and teams are always trying to gauge a player's signability before the draft. They don't want to risk wasting a pick on someone who's probably not going to sign.

Investing in a player is a business transaction, and my organization wants to ensure that they're putting money into someone who can bring value to the team and, just as important, is ready to sign when their name is called on Draft Day.

The Process of Getting Submitted for the Draft

Getting submitted for the draft might seem a bit intimidating at first, but don't worry. I'm here to help you understand and navigate it with confidence. Here's the breakdown.

Scouts monitor promising prospects, creating detailed reports on skills, potential, and character. These reports help organizations make a list of potential draftees, and if a scout thinks you've got what it takes, a cross-checker from their organization might also come to assess you. Sometimes, organizations invite potential draft picks to pre-draft workouts, which is an excellent opportunity for players to show off their skills in front of multiple scouts and decision-makers.

As the draft approaches, scouts have a tough job deciding which players to submit from the many talented individuals they've seen. They rely on a constantly evolving draft list and work closely with their colleagues, exchanging information and discussing potential prospects.

In the final month before the draft, teams meet to finalize their draft list. Scouts from all over the country rank players and create a master list for their organization to use during the draft.

Before the draft, teams hold pre-draft meetings where scouts present their top prospects and share their evaluations with the organization's decision-makers. This collaborative effort helps teams create their draft boards and prioritize potential picks, and it also helps to draw attention to players who may have been overlooked.

When the draft finally arrives, scouts gather to create a master draft board that reflects the consensus among the scouts and the organization. Factors like round, value, role grade, signability, and even internal politics will influence your final position on this list.

When I was with the Brewers, I was one of the first, if not the first, scouts tracking a kid from Leander, TX, named Michael Reed. I watched him at a workout in North Texas and followed him around that summer, seeing him at the big event in Jupiter, FL. Every time I saw him, he just got better and better. He ended up being named one of the top 200 prospects heading into the 2011 draft.

My scouting report had Michael as a second-round pick that year.

I had a great home visit with the Reed family. Michael and his dad, Benton, were being very pragmatic in weighing the potential of going pro vs. moving on to college. It's a big decision. But knowing where a player stands on these issues helps the scout determine a player's signability before heading into the draft room. With the relationship we built that day, I felt comfortable with what I thought it would take for Michael to become a Brewer.

Fast forward to the MLB Draft. I felt Michael belonged in the second round, but it just didn't fit with the organization's overall draft strategy. That's the way it goes sometimes. As we're about to head into the 5th round, I get a call from Brewers Scouting Director Bruce Seid. Getting straight to the point, he says, "Michael Reed, you want him – what's it gonna take?" I said,

"Yeah, I want him. I can get it done for 500k." Bruce says, "All right. If you can get it done, call me back. You have the 500k."

Now, I knew that Michael and his dad wanted more. But I also knew the relationship mattered and that Michael wanted to play professional baseball. So, I got his dad on the phone, "Benton, it's the 5th round, and Michael's in play." He started talking about Michael maybe going to college and their thought process of figuring out what they would need. Out of respect, I wanted to hear him out, but the draft was moving fast, and there just wasn't time. I knew what I could offer, so I jumped in and said, "Benton, what's the final number? Will 500k work?"

After a few seconds, he said, "Yeah. 500k and 100k for school."

The Milwaukee Brewers selected Michael Reed in the 5th round of the 2011 Major League Baseball Draft. He made his Major League debut for the team on September 26, 2015, and went on the play for the Atlanta Braves and San Francisco Giants.

Building that relationship with Michael's family through the home visit process and determining his signability put him on the board for that round. If I didn't think he was signable, somebody else would have been in that spot, and Michael may have never played in the big leagues.

My relationship with the Reeds continues to this day. Even though he is no longer playing baseball, I still talk to Michael and Benton regularly.

Let me step back. You may be reading this and saying, "Wait, what was that 100k for school?"

Sometimes teams may negotiate incentives beyond a signing bonus with players who decide to forgo a college scholarship to enter the MLB draft. It makes their decision less risky if they know they still have a chance at getting a college education when their playing days come to an end.

Every step of this process is an opportunity for you to showcase your skills and passion for the game. Embrace these moments to increase your chances of making it to the big leagues. Make a lasting impression on as many scouts as possible. Put your best foot forward and let your talent shine.

Draft Day

During the MLB draft, teams select amateur baseball players from high schools, colleges, and other amateur baseball clubs.

Until 2022, the modern draft order was based on a team's win-loss records from the previous season, and the team with the worst record picks first.

Starting in 2023, the MLB Draft will use a lottery system for the first six picks, with the three worst teams having the best chance to get the No. 1 pick. All 18 non-playoff teams will participate in the lottery, with their odds based on their records. Teams with revenue-sharing payouts have restrictions on how often they can get lottery picks.

The draft will continue to have 20 rounds. After the first round, non-playoff teams will pick based on their records, while playoff clubs will pick in reverse order of their postseason finish.

The change is an effort to prevent poor-performing teams from the previous season from "tanking" so they would be guaranteed a top-six pick in the next year's draft.

During the 20 rounds, each team has one pick per round. Teams have a limited time, typically around 4 minutes, to make their selection in each round. If a team fails to make a pick within the allotted time, they can still make their selection later, but they risk losing the player to another team.

Each team's representative announces their pick to the MLB Commissioner or designated representative. The selection is recorded, and the player's name is added to the team's draft list.

Prospects expected to be drafted early may be invited to attend the draft in person or participate via video conference. Other prospects will likely follow the draft through various media outlets or live streams. Teams typically contact the selected players shortly after their pick to officially inform them of their selection and discuss the next steps.

Once a player is drafted, the team that selected them holds their signing rights for a set period, usually until the following year's draft. During this time, the team will negotiate a contract with the player or agent. Players drafted from high school may choose to attend college instead of signing immediately. In that case, the player will be eligible for the draft again after completing their junior year or turning 21.

After signing a contract, most drafted players begin their professional careers in the minor leagues, working their way up through various levels before potentially reaching the Major

Leagues. The development process can vary significantly from player to player, with some reaching the Major Leagues quickly while others may take several years.

Post-Draft and Signing Decisions

Players drafted right after high school must decide whether to sign a professional contract or pursue other options, such as playing college baseball. Players and their families should weigh the pros and cons of each choice, considering education, financial stability, and long-term career prospects.

Embarking on a Professional Career

Those who sign a professional contract will embark on a new chapter in their baseball journey. High school players will join the team's minor league system, where they will continue to develop their skills and work toward their ultimate goal: reaching the major leagues.

The MLB draft is an exciting and nerve-wracking experience for high school players and their families as players anxiously wait to hear their names called. Some players may be selected in the early rounds, while others may have to wait longer or not be drafted. I urge players and their families to remain positive and focused, understanding that the draft is just one step in their baseball journey. The entire process, from initial discovery to draft day, is a testament to the player's talent and dedication to the sport.

Chapter 12

Swing for the Fences

There you have it—an under-the-hood look at the world of high school baseball scouting. It's a fascinating mix of teamwork, strategy, and good old-fashioned gut instinct, all in the name of finding the next baseball legend.

By understanding the inner workings of the scouting process, you can help your player better navigate their baseball journey. Recognizing the structure of the process, knowing how scouts find and track players, and appreciating the significance of amateur player stats, your player will be better prepared to showcase their abilities and catch the attention of professional scouts. Keep these insights in mind as you work toward your ultimate goal.

The Power of Passion, Persistence, and Determination

In the world of baseball, passion, persistence, and determination are key ingredients for success.

I want to leave you with a few nuggets of wisdom to guide you along the way so that you never forget that whether your player is ultimately drafted, the experience should indeed have a positive impact on their future and one shared by very few.

Love the Game: Remember that your love for baseball is the fuel that drives your journey. Cherish every moment on the field and allow your passion to be the force that propels you forward.

Embrace the Grind: The road to the big leagues is often paved with challenges, setbacks, and obstacles. Embrace the grind, and use these hardships as opportunities to grow, learn, and develop as a player and person.

Trust the Process: It's natural to want immediate results, but understand that reaching your goals takes time, patience, and commitment. Trust the process and allow yourself to develop at your own pace.

Maintain Balance: As you pursue your baseball dreams, don't neglect other important aspects of your life, such as your education, family, and friendships. A healthy balance will ensure you remain grounded, resilient, and well-rounded.

Stay Committed: No matter how difficult the journey becomes, stay committed to your goals and dreams. Remember why you fell in love with baseball and use that passion to fuel your dedication and drive.

Develop a Growth Mindset: Embrace the idea that you can always improve and grow as a player. Approach every challenge as an opportunity to learn and develop, and never shy away from seeking feedback or asking for help.

Be Persistent: The path to success is rarely a straight line. When faced with setbacks or obstacles, be persistent and keep pushing forward. Those who refuse to give up eventually achieve their goals.

Cultivate Resilience: Develop the ability to bounce back from adversity and failure. Setbacks are a natural part of the journey, so use them as inspiration to come back stronger and more determined than ever.

Believe in Yourself: Be confident in your abilities and trust that you have what it takes to achieve your dreams. Believe in yourself, even when the odds seem stacked against you, and you'll find the strength to overcome any obstacle.

As you step into the batter's box of life, remember that your journey to the big leagues is a marathon, not a sprint. Embrace the process, stay true to your passion, and harness the power of persistence and determination. With hard work, dedication, and a little bit of luck, you may one day find yourself standing on the field, ready to take your place among the legends of the game.

Swing for the fences and never forget that every great journey begins with a single step. Your path to the big leagues awaits, and it's up to you to seize the opportunity and make your dreams a reality. Keep your eye on the ball, stay focused, and always remember to enjoy the ride. The memories, friendships, and lessons learned will truly define your journey and shape the player and person you become.

Made in the USA
Middletown, DE
25 May 2023